DIAMOND DAYS

FINDING CLARITY, CONFIDENCE AND CONTENTMENT IN TURBULENT TIMES

PAUL A CHAPIN

Diamond Days
Copyright © 2018 by Paul A Chapin

Tellwell Talent
www.tellwell.ca

ISBN
978-0-2288-0674-5 (Hardcover)
978-0-2288-0673-8 (Paperback)
978-0-2288-0675-2 (eBook)

CONTENTS

INTRODUCTION

Have you ever had one of those days when everything just flows? The sun is shining, the birds are singing and everything you do works out effortlessly. There's a smile on your face, a lightness to your step and you don't have a care in the world. Your entire world seems perfectly synched and you feel powerfully connected to it all. You are performing at peak and life has wrapped you in a warm soft layer of contentment. This is a diamond day.

I've been having a lot of diamond days lately, and they seem to be improving in depth and frequency. Even my non-diamond days have improved. I owe it all to these eight codes and the practices outlined in this book. If you've ever experienced days like these and crave more of them then this book is for you. If you've never experienced a diamond day, this book is definitely for you.

We are living through a very interesting period in human history. The rise of nationalism, the degradation of our natural environment, the ongoing brutality of war, religious extremism, and the deeply divisive nature of political discourse. And that's a slow news day when there's time for a puppy story.

There has never been a better time to examine and embrace what is truly important. In this critical period when greed trumps integrity and power overwhelms decency, the world can seem a bit chaotic and heavy. Now is a great time to slow down and reevaluate our perspectives, and choices. Individually it is possible to create our own peace and order from this turmoil. Collectively even greater things are possible.

This was never going to be a book; this was a way to clarify and reflect on my own process as I worked through a uniquely challenging period in my life. I was the lab rat in my own little experiment, and it wasn't until I saw results that I thought to share. I can attest to the effectiveness of these practices because I also do them. Improvement comes daily and has made a huge difference in terms of my clarity, calmness, and overall happiness. My only regret is that somebody didn't give me this book years ago.

How did I get here? Basically, I did a lot of reading, my interest grew, and I moved into some deliberate actions to test that material. I succeeded, failed, learned and progressed. Eventually, I got to a place where things started to click. The further I went the easier it became. Life became simpler, and I found myself getting calmer, clearer and happier. In my growing enthusiasm, I started to build a simple framework to condense the knowledge and practice into some basic codes and actions. This book is my best attempt at that framework. In many ways, it became a marriage of common practicality and universal awareness.

Normally, this type of book would outline a principle and then encourage specific actions in support of that principle before moving on to the next. I went another way. The first section outlines the specific codes before moving into the actions in the following section. I have a couple of reasons for this. First, I want readers to gain a solid feel for the codes and deal with any potential shifts in perspective before moving forward. Second, and probably more important, not all actions correlate directly to a specific code. The lines get a little blurry, and some of the actions will support multiple codes.

Your time is your most valuable and finite resource; out of respect, I have kept this material as brief as I possibly could. Welcome to Diamond Days. May you find your own diamond days within these pages.

PART I

THE EIGHT CODES

In this context, codes are a system of principles guiding behavior. As I have read and reflected, I have come to understand that the following codes are universal in nature, tending to transcend the more rigid rules we have come to know as law. These are commonly referenced in countless texts dating back hundreds of years and show up in differing versions throughout our history. Why eight? I'd love to tell you it's a mystical connection to the symbol for infinity, but it merely worked out that way. It was not intentional, at least not on my part.

As we review the following codes and actions, it may be helpful to consider the idea of connected themes. All these codes and actions are interconnected in some way. Themes to consider include awareness, choice, connection, mortality and time, the same themes that tend to run through our lives. We can review them further in the final section.

The Code of Duality

DUALITY. When we build our universal awareness, we find calmness, balance, and confidence. In this state, we make better choices.

We are each two entities. "We are not human beings having a spiritual experience, we are spiritual beings having a human experience." While the source of this quote has been disputed and debated, it should not distract us from the message. We are both human and spiritual to our core. Accepting our duality is the key to building universal awareness, and universal awareness gives us the foundational strength and confidence to create our most fulfilling life.

We need not be followers of religious doctrine to embrace the idea of spirit. We can share the belief of spirit without the peripheral rules and rituals if we so choose. The entity we will discover is lighter, freer, unburdened by human constructs, and open to huge possibilities. As we gain knowledge of the spirit, we also gain insight into how our human and spiritual sides interact.

Human

The majority of us are most familiar with our human side. This side is the "us" we know the best. It's the combination of our experiences, knowledge, and thoughts. Our human side is our physical presence including the things we have or haven't done to maintain it. It's our opinions and judgments and, when we look deeper, the beliefs and values we hold as a result.

Our human side includes the entire range of emotions we experience as we act or react to the world around us. It's also our reaction to those emotions, judgments, and opinions from others. Our human side includes the defensive and offensive mechanisms we have adopted to keep ourselves safe.

It's the choices we've made to either conform or rebel. It's our successes and failures. Sometimes it's the mask that we wear. In many ways, it has evolved into a role that we play, whether it's a role we've chosen or one chosen for us. It is, above all, fallible and sometimes flawed.

As we play our human role, we expend energy in making judgments and forming opinions. This is right or wrong. This is good or bad. This helps and that hurts. These judgments apply to people, situations, and, most harshly, to ourselves. When we make judgments or form opinions, we may take action. We will defend and justify these judgments or opinions to others. Sometimes these judgments are important to our life; sometimes they're not.

As we move through life we make decisions and choices. Sometimes, as we may have learned in school, they are win/win decisions. Sometimes only we win. Sometimes we win and someone else loses. Sometimes we lose.

We also build relationships. Some are positive and cherished. Some are familiar but casual. Some we outright avoid. When we build relationships, we often gravitate to those who share our beliefs and avoid those who don't. We are not always conscious of making this distinction.

We have egos and our egos influence our decisions, judgments, opinions and choices. The influence of ego tends to be negative, and we may expend effort and energy to keep it in check. Occasionally, it gets away from us.

We acquire wealth, and it feels important. Some of it we use to buy things that make our lives easier and more enjoyable. Some of it we give away, and some of it we put away. It serves as both a trending and comparative score-card. It tells us how we're doing in life.

Spirit

Our spiritual sides are very different. Our spirit sees life as a game. It approaches the game with the purity and curiosity of a wide-eyed innocent. It almost can't believe it gets to play such an amazing game with its twists and turns, multiple plotlines, and unpredictable outcomes. Our spirit approaches the game with pure joy and excite-ment, on the edge of its seat in anticipation of the next move, direction or outcome. And while it's engaged in the wild craziness of the whole thing, it's less concerned with the result. Our spirit is just grateful to play and knows it ends the same for everyone anyway. Game over, please play again in another dimension.

While it is pure innocence, it is also pure wisdom. It remembers the important things our human side may have forgotten along the way. It remembers the importance of nature, the bond we share with all creatures, including humans, and how we strengthen those bonds with kindness.

Our spirit tends not to think in absolutes. It doesn't process issues of right or wrong but in observable differences. It's more interested in the why than the what; it's a student of human behavior. It understands the heavy cost of judgment, not only on those being judged but on the judges themselves. Similarly, it understands the cost of defending against judgments in terms of time, energy and health. It refuses to engage in these activities. It simply doesn't see the point and, besides, the whole judgment thing distracts from the joy of play.

It travels light and fast. It attaches less importance to stuff than our human side. Our spirit tries to avoid too many possessions for fear they become only a load to carry. It finds that a lot of stuff ultimately slows the game and tends to make it one dimensional. When it leaves the game, it will travel extremely light and fast.

It participates in making choices. If it gets its way it wants to run those choices through some simple filters. In fact, it's quite inflexible on this point like a petulant child. Its primary filter is "do no harm."

The spiritual us has no ego and almost seems confused or amused with the concept of self. The spirit exists as an extension of the universe, part of an overall collective that has connection to all things. From this bond, it makes connections effortlessly.

Unencumbered by judgment or opinion, the spirit seeks connection with a much wider variety of humans. It seems like it would meet everybody if it could. The spirit wants to extend its connection to the human level. It understands that diversity adds richness to the game.

Interaction

Our human and spiritual sides seem to be engaged in mutual learning. The spirit is deeply interested in the human experience and has been from the start. Although it learns without judgment or opinion, it is curious. No doubt there is much to find interesting.

As humans, many of us have really only started to learn about our spiritual side, and we have some catching up to do. The most important thing we learn is that the spirit exists on a much higher plane. It is as divine and intelligent as the universe to which it's connected. As we gain competency in connecting to our spiritual side, we gain access to that intelligence as well. As we carefully get over the initial clumsiness of that connection process, we are able to function more and more on that elevated plane.

What is available to us here is calmness, clarity, and confidence. In general, we feel more powerful and centered when we approach life from a spiritual center. The turbulence and waves that normally hammer us as we move through life are more likely to pass under us with little effect. The turbulence still happens; we just build the capability to ride over it. It's not so much about changing our world as changing the way we deal with it. And yet by achieving those changes, we can ultimately change our world.

Most of us have only a limited awareness of our spirit, since we have led our lives primarily from our human identity. As we learn and progress, we can defer more and more to the spirit for guidance. It's a lot like having our own built-in coach, an instant and ready source of wisdom. And while they may eventually morph into one, this distinction at the outset aids in learning and growth.

So, here is the big question. How can we be certain of the existence of a universal power and, by extension, a spirit? The better question is "how can we not?" Once we choose to look, the clues are everywhere.

They are found in piles of literature written by some very wise and enlightened authors. They are showcased in the inherent intelligence of nature with its perfect synchronicity. They show up in our own intuition as we become competent in the practice of meditation, and learn to sit in silence with our thoughts.

Granted, as a lifelong skeptic, I can tell you even these clues are inconclusive. At best, we have a circumstantial argument. As the cliché goes, "the jury could go either way." So, after all the reading, learning to meditate, witnessing the magic of nature, listening to our gut and practicing silence there is still one thing left to do.

We have to leap. For the skeptics among us, there is an act of faith we need to close the deal. Eventually, we have to take a position on the truth of the whole thing. If we wait for the sudden appearance of a Jedi or some robed messenger, we may be waiting a long time. Commitments like these can certainly feel like some big deal.

I can tell you from my own experience, it is the easiest part of the program. Accepting the case for universal wisdom is effortless and for good reason. There is no downside, risk, or safety hazard. By comparison, the upside is huge. It is simply the final piece to the puzzle — the final item on our to-do list. Buy groceries, fill up the car, and accept we have a spiritual side connected to a higher power. It really is that easy.

I don't want to dwell on this too long. It's starting to feel a bit like a lecture on spirituality, and that is not my intent. This is about leveraging some basic knowledge to improve the richness and enjoyment of living. As I've been writing, I have been mulling a question in the back of my mind. Is it really necessary to accept the duality of our existence in order to successfully implement the following practices? Ultimately, I believe it helps; there is value here, regardless, but it goes much deeper when we accept the case for universal wisdom.

I'm not going to get a six-pack doing one set of sit-ups, and I'm not going to gain competency by trying these practices once. Operating from a basic understanding of universal wisdom is what gets me through the trials and errors of practice. Somewhere inside, I need to know this will work. Willpower alone won't get it done.

This whole process is as much about the why as the what. Why do we achieve a state of calm and clarity when we do these things? Much of the underlying value in this approach comes from strengthening a connection to the higher power of the universe. If we can't believe in it, we simply can't connect to it.

The Code of Constructs

CONSTRUCTS. There is no right or wrong way to navigate the world of human constructs. We can make our own rules.

Our spiritual side exists in, and is connected to, the natural universe. Its natural habitat is Mother Nature as we experience it here on Earth. This habitat consists of the atmosphere, vegetation, terrain, and all living species. For argument's sake, let's say it represents half of the world we experience; although in reality, it's a much smaller percentage for many of us city dwellers. For now, let's look at the other half.

As humans have emerged the dominant species on the planet, we have sought to tame and control our environment. Through these efforts, we have developed ideas, products, infrastructure, rules, methods, and cultural guidelines. Other than the natural universe, all things we now experience in life are made up: they are human constructs. The things we own, the things we do, the institutes we deal with all began as an idea in some person's head. Some of these ideas were quite clever and others perhaps not so much.

What is available to us from this perspective? Pretty much everything. Every method or product that has ever been thought or invented can be rethought, reinvented or replaced completely. In fact, it's almost guaranteed they will be; it's simply a matter of time. They are both fabricated and temporary.

This leads us to an inevitable truth. When it comes to life, there is no right or wrong way to do something, and if there were, nobody would know it anyway. Sometimes we assume they do. "What do we do?" We will probably hear a guess. "I don't know, let's follow the tall guy. He seems to know what he's doing." Chances are he doesn't. A better choice is to find our own authentic path.

Rules

Webster defines a rule as: "A regulation or bylaw governing procedure or controlling conduct." Rules are human constructs designed with the specific intent of controlling other humans. Often rules are helpful in our society, other times they're not.

The rule of law in society is generally (not always) helpful in protecting citizens from harm. When nefarious elements in our society seek to harm us through criminal or civil transgressions, the law is designed to assist us and to keep order (specifically in a democratic society).

Sometimes rules are used to maintain queues: the system can't handle demand and employs rules to delay users. Often, they are designed to push the workload to the user. Fill out this form, jump through this hoop, and do this thing the system used to do for you. They are another form of behavior control.

In many cases, we see rules that have outlived their usefulness. They are obsolete. This tends to happen in older institutions. We've all dealt with nonsensical policies and those who defend them in the face of reason.

In truth, they exist everywhere. Either through intention or neglect, the evolution of these rules has not kept pace with our social evolution.

The rules we really need to address and challenge are more in the area of cultural norms. These are often rules designed to impede our progress in life and maintain class, gender or race distinction. Sometimes these are referred to as "frightened old white men rules." They are designed to maintain the status quo, ensure an adequate supply of worker bees, and keep the general populace in line. They are an invisible force field that exists mostly in our minds.

In some ways, these norms combine the worst of obsolete rules with queueing rules. They tend to state that progress from Point A to Point B must take place on a specific path or a finite number of paths. The messaging includes such advice as knowing your place, pay your dues and respect tradition. The path to the C suite starts in the mailroom. Start small and build your business slowly. Go to medical school before performing open heart surgery — OK, we should probably keep that one.

In Western society, we are in the early stages of seeing these rules disrupted and obliterated. In the business world, we are seeing the emergence of a shared economy, solopreneurs, and entire sectors that didn't exist even five years ago. People who want to operate at Point B are starting at Point B. Early adopters are stepping over the old rules and making their own. While this disruption is primarily a grassroots phenomenon, it will eventually change our larger institutions or render them redundant. In some cases, it already has.

We need to understand the implications. Change is flying at us, and we need to come to terms with that reality. It is likely to get a bit messy. If rapid change makes us uncomfortable, we need to find a way to get comfortable. If it excites us, let's embrace the idea we can make our own rules.

The Code of Non-Judgment

NON-JUDGMENT. When we practice non-judgment, our lives become lighter and freer. We have energy to pursue more productive things.

Our human selves are deeply engaged in the act of judgment. It's a pastime for some, an obsession for others, and a way of life for most. Most of us make dozens of judgments each day. We've become so adept at it, we often don't even notice. We pass judgment on other humans, ourselves, and most of our daily situations.

While we don't notice we are spending much of our day in judgment, we also don't notice the damage it does. It steals our most precious commodity of time. It tends to suck the energy out of our lives, it feels so tiring. If pushed too far, it can affect our physical and mental health. In self-judgment, we can find all kinds of reasons to live small. Ultimately, it can distract us from building great lives. It's quite a challenge building our own lives when we're busy judging others.

Judgment is at the heart of human conflict. It is what divides us. In fact, it's virtually impossible to be in conflict with another without first having judged them. The judgment creates an opinion. The opinion comes with an emotional attachment. The more intense the emotion, the nastier that conflict is likely to be. If the judgment and resulting opinion are positive, we will eventually encounter somebody who disagrees with our assessment, and that quickly, we are back in conflict.

Most of the issues we judge are, frankly, none of our business. As a Pareto head, I'm going to tell you that applies to at least 80 % of the issues or people we encounter on any given day. Imagine how much smoother our lives would be if we could eliminate even 80 % of that useless junk from our brain.

Nowhere is judgment becoming nastier these days than in politics. Here's the thing (there's always a thing): we live in a democracy. Every four years we get to vote for the person, party or platform we believe will create a positive living environment. While the system may have flaws, it sure beats the alternative.

The time between elections is increasingly filled with deeply divisive and deliberately outrageous provocative discourse. Political provocation has become something of a global sport. Most of the provocateurs don't even believe the vitriol they spew, although they gleefully watch the response they trigger. People are reeled in by the millions on all sides of issues. The end result of this discourse is, well, nothing good.

For most of us, the only real influence we have on the process is to vote. If we choose to engage in the interim discourse, we should do so with an understanding of the cost to our health and enjoyment of life. The only way to understand the toll is to unplug and disengage from political discourse for a while. As our energy improves, I'm willing to bet we won't go back.

Self-judgment

Where we really need to lighten up is in our self-judgment. As tough as we are on others, the efforts pale in comparison to how we sometimes treat ourselves. Left unchecked, that negative little voice inside our heads that convinces us to live safe and small can do a lot of damage. The consistent messaging includes things like we're not good enough, or it's not safe.

In coaching, we call that voice the saboteur. A good coach will help the client recognize the voice of the saboteur. Together they name the voice, agree that it doesn't belong in the coaching conversation, and return to working on the client's goals. With a bit of repetition, the client learns to dismiss the voice without assistance. The saboteur masquerades as our buddy. It will convince us it's there to keep us "safe". The bigger we play, the harder it works.

Years ago, I suffered a spinal cord injury that paralyzed the lower half of my body. A few months later, with a lot of luck and some excellent care, I walked out of the hospital with the aid of a couple of canes. I had been an avid skier and, somehow in a moment of optimism, I equated those canes to ski poles. Suffice to say, the ensuing experiment was an epic failure. Several years later, friends convinced me to try again. The battle to train my body was nothing compared to the battle I had with my mind. The internal conversation went something like this:

Buddy, I'm telling you skiing is a bad idea. You don't want to get paralyzed again. Who's going to scratch your nose? All right, I see you're determined, but let's stay down here on the bunny hill. That big hill looks pretty steep to me. OK, we're on the big chair, just promise me you'll stick to the greens. Dude, that's a blue! It's way too steep! OK, you're focused I respect that, just be really careful and ski slow. Woah, what are you doing? That's the black diamond of death. You can't ski that, they'll never find your body!

And on and on it went. The further I went, the harder it tried to push back. The more success I achieved, the weaker and more ridiculous it became. Eventually, it became silent, although it still returns from time to time.

To diminish its hold, we need to recognize it, name it, treat it with some humor (or disdain if we prefer), and push on through to our bigger life. The process becomes a skill like any other. The more we practice, the stronger we become.

At the risk of being overly obvious, this is a technique. The voice is that part of us that has existed over thousands of years to keep us safe. It's the same one that told our ancestors not to fight a saber-tooth tiger with a small stick, and there are still times we need to heed the advice. It's our conscious choices that guide us to those messages we should either heed or ignore.

Situational judgment

Obviously, some situational judgments are necessary to navigate life. "If I step in front of that bus, it's going to leave a mark" is probably a wise judgment to make. Others are traps more likely to drag us into the same energy sucking, time-wasting activity.

The most common of these is the fairness or justice trap. Sometimes life's not fair, the universe doesn't care, and neither should we. Thankfully, progress in life is rarely if ever linear. That would create a snooze fest. A healthier response is to consider the possibility of something better on the horizon. In surfing vernacular our set is still out there. It's OK to visit brief moments of disappointment; we just can't live there. We can examine the disappointing event to see if there's a lesson, or choose to step over it. It's really just a choice.

Another common trap is the outcome prediction. We judge a situation and predict all manner of potential outcomes, none of them good. In almost every case our crystal ball malfunctions and our predictions fail to materialize. All we are left with is the unnecessary stress. The practice we need is to stay in the moment and accept the future will unfold as the universe intended. It's best to identify and disrupt the thought pattern as quickly as we notice it happening. A simple acknowledgment of our poor prediction skills should help.

A trickier one is the projection trap. It might start with a thought like, "that ass is judging me." (Notice the irony in this picture.) Actually, no, we're judging them. In fact, there's a high probability they're not considering us at all since they're too busy with their own lives. In those rare instances when our assessment might be true, a reasonable response is usually, "OK, it's really none of my business." If we have the time, we can pause to address the cause, or step over it and continue with our day. Again, it's a matter of choice.

Finally, there's the "this has nothing to do with me, but I'm going to judge it anyway" trap. We find material for this on the six o'clock news or social media. We can satisfy our desire to stay informed by replacing judgment with more detached curiosity. With the information observed, we may even identify a way to improve the situation of others. Of course, we'll need to act rather than merely adding our voice to the white noise of opinion. That should put us back on our mission.

You may have noticed something about this section. It's pretty much common sense. You might even be thinking, "Yup everybody knows this." This may be true, although some days I have questions. One of those questions is "if everybody knows this, why do we still have some much judgment and conflict in the world?" It's simply not enough to know; we must also act.

The Code of Defenselessness

DEFENSELESSNESS. When we refuse to defend ourselves to others, we find calmness and grace.

Closely tied to judgment is the practice of defensiveness. When we perceive we're on the receiving end of judgment, our instinct is to defend ourselves. It's possible we spend even more time defending than judging. We are certainly more passionate about it since it involves that most precious entity of self.

Responsibility

As we defend ourselves, we sometimes take the position that things are not our fault. Logically, if the fault is not ours, it lies with somebody else. Our arguments are often crafted to absolve ourselves of responsibility. This can become a problem when we start to believe that narrative.

Each of us must take absolute responsibility for the current state of our lives. All our past opinions, beliefs, choices, and actions have contributed to our present reality. If we can't own that, we run the risk of inertia, an inability to move forward. The mindset becomes "somebody else got me here, somebody has to get me out." That just won't work. The freedom we feel from living a victim narrative is actually a huge prison. It can be a seductive but damaging mindset. In effect, we give away the power over our lives to those we blame.

Once we embrace that truth, the best thing we can do, ironically, is let it go. The past can't be changed and is a distant distortion of our memory. We have learned the central lesson; the rest is mind junk. Taking responsibility gives us one less reason to defend, and gives us permission to move forward with our lives.

Breaking out of a victim narrative often requires an act of forgiveness. Too many of us refuse to forgive. We believe forgiveness lets our offender off the hook when it actually lets ourselves off the hook. The act of forgiveness says we refuse to carry our resentment because feelings of resentment block us from living our most fulfilling life. Forgiveness is an act of self-healing that has very little to do with our offender. To live our best life, we should learn to forgive.

Fitting In

Our drive to defend ourselves comes from a need to receive validation and approval from others. Our desire to fit in is a learned response reinforced through years of schooling and career. We weren't born with it, and it certainly isn't a spiritual response. Here's a great example of what fitting in really does for us.

Some years ago NASA contracted Dr. George Land to develop a creativity test for their scientists and engineers.

The test was designed to measure creative potential and was deemed a success by both NASA and Dr. Land. Curious about whether creativity was learned or acquired, they gave the same test to a group of children. While tests of this nature are always open to questions of subjectivity, it was the trend that caught them off guard.

They tested 1,600 children aged four to five, and an incredible 98 % scored at the genius level for creativity. Five years later, they gave the same children the same test. This time, only 30 % scored at the genius level. Five years after that only 12 % scored at the same genius level. Subsequent testing revealed that only 2 % of adults score at that level. While we can concede that causality wasn't proven in this experiment, it gives pause for reflection. Our society and its institutions seem to excel at beating the creativity out of ourselves.

Sometimes when we choose our own path through life, we elicit a response from those around us. People may become confused, maybe frightened, sometimes aggressive, and usually judgmental. From time to time, we may be tempted to defend our decisions and choices. We need to resist that temptation. It's a huge time and energy waster that is likely to lead us nowhere. We are better served by trusting our instincts.

We may also notice that some people become less "available" as they deal with their discomfort. We need to view this as a positive development. This creates space for others who may be more supportive or challenging as we move forward in life. People will move in and out of our lives at different times and for different reasons. We need to make peace with that dynamic.

We should also be aware if we are projecting our own discomfort onto others. Sometimes we assume people are uncomfortable with our decisions, when, in fact, we may be dealing with our own discomfort. What we initially see as external judgment may actually be the voice of our own saboteur. As we develop skill with our instincts and listening to our bodies, we can identify and address those instances.

Failure

If I could ban one word from the English language, that word would be failure. It's a word that evokes pure terror in large swathes of the population. It crushes big dreams before they start. It is the nastiest eff word in our language.

Failure is nothing more than validation of effort. It only happens when we try, when we move forward with our lives and push beyond previous limits. Failure is where our deepest learning happens. It should be cherished, celebrated and sought out. It requires no defense or explanation.

The Code of Acceptance

ACCEPTANCE. We are right where we should be. Be grateful and present.

A critical component to finding our diamond days can be summed up in this simple yet powerful statement: "Things are as they should be." Each of us is right where we should be in this moment in time. In this moment, we can be most effective by being both present and grateful.

This does not mean we sit back and let life happen to us. We still strive. We still look for opportunities to grow, to learn and to evolve. We still seek ways to add value and be helpful to ourselves, our families, our communities and our employers or customers. In a state of acceptance, we are more focused, less distracted and better equipped to stay on task, regardless of the nature of that task.

Acceptance is more about dropping our attachment to a predetermined result. Don't take this the wrong way, but the universe is much smarter than us. It makes no sense to attach ourselves to an outcome when there is a good chance the universe has a better one. Life won't always give us what we want, but it will give us what we need. Rigidly holding to our intended result in the face of all reason is a sure path to disappointment and unhappiness.

Any time we take action on a situation or issue, that issue becomes dynamic; our action causes that issue to change. Often we can predict the change based on our previous experience and learning. Sometimes, though, that change is unexpected. It takes us in a new direction. This is particularly true when we are pushing past our previous limits of experience or knowledge. It's like flowing water. Sometimes it will follow the channel we want, and sometimes it's determined to take a new channel.

At the moment we discover the new direction, we have a choice to make. We can choose to explore the new direction, or we can exert force and effort to maintain our original course. In the water analogy, we might have to pull out the heavy equipment. To exert our will we might have to build a dam, dig a new channel back to the old channel or even change the elevation. It's likely to cost us time, effort and resources.

Or we can choose to follow the new direction. Although this is the path of least effort, it may be the path of most value. It's probably a path the universe has offered us. It may be the path where we find our highest energy, the most richness, satisfaction, and happiness. Even if it isn't, even if we've somehow misread the signs so what? Along that path, new ones will be revealed. Life is about the paths. It's our journey that matters. Hopefully, we're in no rush to reach the destination.

What the universe can bring to this process is creativity, flexibility and a level of uncertainty that makes things fun, interesting and playful. When we connect to the universe through our spiritual side, it becomes a form of co-creation. We work in collaboration with the universe to create whatever project has our focus. In these moments we achieve the feeling of flow that can be simultaneously tranquil and exciting.

Past Present and Future

Of the three tenses of time, only one is real and relevant. Do we believe tomorrow is relevant? For approximately 151,600 of us, there is no tomorrow; today is the last day on the planet. What about the past? We don't remember it accurately, and we couldn't change it even if we did. The only moment we have, the only moment that is real is the one we are experiencing right now. The only place life ever happens is in the here and now.

For many of us "right now" is being wasted either regretting the past or worrying about the future. The past is irrelevant. If there was a lesson to learn, we've already learned it. How will we handle the events of tomorrow? Like rock stars because we always have, and we are still standing. Now let's get back to experiencing this moment with our breath, our senses, and our emotions while immersed in our surroundings. This is life — and now it's gone.

How would those 151,600 people approach today if they knew? Would they be present? Would their senses be a little sharper? Would they hug their loved ones a little tighter or linger in the sunlight a little longer? Make no mistake, we are those people, and we owe it to ourselves to live that way.

Gratitude

Today is a gift deserving of our gratitude. The fact that we are here to experience it at all is the biggest gift. We have each beaten tremendous odds just to achieve existence. Gratitude goes much further and deeper than winning the genetic lottery. We can and should be grateful for all our experiences, the people we have met, the things we've owned, the food we've eaten and the air we've breathed. The list is infinite.

Sadly, many of us are so fixated on "what's next" we've forgotten to appreciate "what's now." We need to slow down and honor the things, people and experiences we have already received. One day the answer to "what's next" is going to be one of those bad news/good news scenarios. "Unfortunately, today is moving day — the good news is you don't have to pack."

The Code of Detachment

DETACHMENT. We are much more than our transitory wealth or bestowed titles

Apparently, there has been a persistent and troubling shortage of automobiles in our world. I did not know. And it's not only cars. There are signs we are in imminent danger of running out of all consumer products. The evidence is everywhere. Available until Friday! Buy now before they're gone! These deals won't last! Scarcity is just another human invention. Its primary purpose is to manipulate and control human behavior.

The universe doesn't understand scarcity; it is by nature infinitely abundant. Even here on this crowded tiny blue dot we call home, the universe is capable of providing for its billions of human inhabitants. It isn't the production system that's flawed; it's our distribution system that is failing. The root cause of this failure is our constructed scarcity bias that drives fear, greed and hoarding behavior. In a scarcity mindset, we believe we must choose between rewarding achievement and finding a basic level of comfort for all beings. In an abundant universe, both states are possible.

Wealth in Context

We are not put on Earth to hoard wealth. Hoarding wealth for its own sake is a fear-based activity based on a scarcity mentality. Hoarding wealth inhibits the natural state of flow, and flow is one of the fundamental codes of the universe.

Money is called currency for a very good reason: it is meant to flow. Money was invented to facilitate trade. With currency, our ancestors didn't have to physically trade the chair they had built for the chicken they wanted. Money's value comes from what it represents. In and of itself it has no value. It's just a piece of paper or, more commonly, bits and bytes in a virtual world. For proof, we could visit Venezuela where we'd need a suitcase of the stuff to buy a loaf of bread. We would want to learn carpentry or, better yet, poultry farming. If we think that can't elsewhere, we're not paying attention.

We are the temporary custodians of wealth, no matter how large or small. In terms of universal time, each of us is here for a brief moment. From this perspective, the concept of ownership is a bit absurd. At best, we are long-term renters; we are not leaving here with any of it.

Wealth itself is neither positive nor negative. It tends to become negative when we begin to associate our self-worth with our level of wealth, or the made-up titles we may receive from time to time. I remember once being given the title Strategic Development Officer. Cool, I thought, I wonder what that is. It turned out to be corporate strategy, business development, supply chain and IT — basically, every department nobody else wanted. But it was still a very cool title.

When we connect our personal identities with any wealth or bestowed titles, we give away our power to those possessions. We should remember they are both fabricated and temporary. We are more than our business cards or bank accounts — much more. We can chase them if it amuses us, but we should maintain a perspective of detachment. These things will come and go. With detachment we guard against any feelings of loss, and mourning the loss of made-up stuff is only more brain junk.

Heroes

As a society, we used to admire the builders and creators. Our heroes were those entrepreneurial individuals who pushed through the envelope of possibilities to create new realities. As their achievements grew so did their bank accounts. The line between achievement and wealth became a little blurry. It gets blurrier when the wealth is passed to subsequent generations.

For some of us, the focus of admiration has shifted through this evolution. We become a little less focused on the achievements and maybe too much focused on the wealth. Great achievement may be worthy of admiration, great wealth not so much. We should practice some care when choosing our heroes and those we may wish to emulate. Wealth and achievement are not always connected. Neither are wealth and happiness.

When chasing wealth becomes our primary focus, we never seem to find enough. The chase never ends and happiness remains elusive. When we chase achievement through our own creativity, wealth seems to find us. If we accept it with gratitude, our happiness is virtually guaranteed.

Let's be our own heroes. We can all be heroes with the right focus. If we do it because it creates value, because we love it, because it has meaning, because it helps or because it leaves a powerful and positive legacy, then we're probably doing it for the right reasons.

Tools or Jewels

It's not more stuff that brings us happiness, it is having fewer wants. For amusement, I compiled a list of stuff I couldn't live without. Not surprisingly that list was very short. For a filter, I used the tools versus jewels distinction. Tools are those things that actually enhance my functionality and enjoyment of life. Jewels are those things that just make me look more impressive to the world. If you're interested, here's my list:

- About 10 % of my current inventory of clothes
- Some electronics (iPod, phone and notebook)
- My ski equipment
- My mountain bike
- A place to live
- Some furniture and dishes
- A vehicle (I live on the Canadian prairie where you can spend days watching your dog run away.)

Subtract items I can just rent, and the list becomes a few clothes and electronics (although, you'll have to pry the skis and bike out of my cold, dead hands). Completing this exercise improved my perspective and created a feeling of lightness. Try it.

I am very fortunate to live within an hour of one of the most beautiful and majestic parks on the planet. I can visit and enjoy Banff National Park for very little if any cost. On the other hand, I will never have enough money to buy it. This knowledge in no way lessens my enjoyment. My enjoyment is actually higher; I'm not burdened with the responsibility of maintaining a massive park. The same holds true for most of life's experiences.

Please don't misunderstand. I'm not saying don't buy nice stuff. If you have the means, knock yourself out; stuff is fun, and it brings moments of joy. (If you lack the means, don't even think about it; that's a path to misery and financial slavery — different book). We should embrace every opportunity to experience fun and joy in our lives. Joy achieved through stuff comes with a caveat; it usually doesn't last long.

People will tell you that Western society is preoccupied or even obsessed with acquiring stuff. I tend to disagree.

I believe that deep down most people understand that stuff, while fun, isn't all that important. However, buying stuff is easier and safer than looking a bit deeper into their lives. And, of course, the people who sell stuff are more than happy to reinforce that safe and easy path.

While building personal wealth for its own sake can feel empty, so might leaving a large inheritance to our off-spring. We should balance our natural desire to help with some common sense. We don't want to rob anybody of the chance to build their own legacy of achievement, and we certainly don't need more entitlement in the universe.

The Code of Choice

CHOICES. When we make choices through filters that do no harm to ourselves, others or our environment, we find harmony. Always choose good health.

Sometimes, it seems life is an endless series of choices we make for ourselves. In many ways, it is. From the moment we leave our childhood homes until the day we move on, we are immersed in the process of choosing. Gaining control over our choices is one of the defining characteristics of our passage into adulthood. For such an important and prevalent process, we know very little about it. Society doesn't do much to prepare us for a life of choices.

Some of the choices we make are big and may have far-reaching consequences. These tend to be issues such as where we live, what we do, and with whom. Will we live in the country or a city? Should it be the tropics or the mountains? What will we study? What about our career? Should we get married and to whom? These are the major choices that tend to send us off into a general direction of focus.

Sometimes, our choices seem much smaller. What should we eat? Should we watch the game or go for a workout?

Attend a social event or spend a quiet evening at home? Even the smaller choices we make create ripples in our lives. If we've ever met a good friend or significant other at a social event or noticed our clothes getting a little snug, then we've experienced those ripples. Our small choices require attention as well.

Choosing not to choose is also a choice. Sometimes, it is the worst choice we can make. I remember the first time I witnessed real poverty. There was a large family near our childhood home living in a complete wreck of a house. They had no electricity or running water, wore rags for clothes and often went without food. Being young, curious, and somewhat indelicate I asked what happened.

The father had once been a prosperous and skilled driller in a local mine. When the mine eventually closed, as mines tend to do, most of his coworkers picked up and moved to new communities and jobs. He chose to stay. He liked where he lived and was convinced the mine would reopen. Of course, it never did. The consequences of that single decision and the reluctance to change it sent heartbreaking ripples through that family that are probably still felt today. Sorry, but not all stories are uplifting.

Stories of others can be helpful in building our own, though. We don't have to make all the mistakes ourselves to learn from them. One of the lessons we could learn is that most choices are reversible or at least changeable into new directions. In the case of the miner, we may assume a certain level of rigidity in his decision-making process. Why else would he have endured those years of misery? Some people wear their commitment to choices as a badge of honor. It can be a very costly badge.

For some of us, the process of choosing is filled with anxiety and stress. In the extreme, the anxiety creates a complete absence of mobility. We reach that proverbial fork in the road and instead of choosing a direction, we awkwardly stand there, sometimes for our entire lives. It may be helpful to understand there are no right or wrong decisions (within reason), they merely have different consequences. If those consequences don't meet our personal requirements, we modify our path. In the case of the miner, his choice may have been acceptable had he chosen to retrain for another profession, start a small enterprise or become a commuter.

Filters

To aid us in making better choices certain tools become very useful. The best of these are filters. Filters are a simple series of questions we can apply to any choice or decision. They are driven by our personal values. When we prepare them ahead of time, they become a ready and critical resource to our decision-making process. While they may vary somewhat from person to person, there are three important filters we should all be using.

Will this choice harm me? What a different world this would be if everyone employed this filter. For starters, we could eliminate all the misery related to substance abuse. Preventative maintenance would be at the forefront of health care. We would all make healthier choices leading to the eradication of at least half of chronic disease. There would be countless other benefits related to harmony, achievement, and happiness. Unfortunately, we can't make these choices for all humanity. We can, at a minimum, choose these things for ourselves.

Will this choice harm others? If we make a choice that benefits ourselves while causing harm to others, it is a bad choice — period. We have probably all done it at some point in our lives. It may not even have been intentional. It still needs to stop, and this is the filter that gets us there.

Will this choice harm our environment? We all need clean air, water and food to thrive. A civilization that threatens its own existence through the destruction of the very environment it needs to survive can't really be considered intelligent. If we can't make a meaningful contribution to the improvement of our natural environment, we should at least not be part of the problem. Again, we can't make this choice for humanity, but we can make it for ourselves.

Intuition

When we immerse in the process of choice, we usually rely on our conscious thoughts to make the decision. As we use our mind to make choices, we tend to improve the quality of our choices over time. Although our decisions tend to improve by degree, choices made by mind alone remain prone to error.

There is another less understood but more powerful tool available to us. That tool is intuition. While the mind is subject to bias and external influences, intuition can be much more stable and accurate. We are each born intuitive beings, although we seem to lose the skill over time. Intuition is not highly valued in our society and is even mocked in some circles. We are taught to value the thinking processes of science and logic over the less understood skill of intuition. Like most neglected skills it becomes dormant over time. The good news is we can reconnect with our intuitive skills with a little knowledge and some intentional effort and practice.

With conscious thought, we eventually learn to make good choices. When we use basic filters that do no harm, those choices become stronger. When we introduce intuition to the process, we push our choices to new and powerful levels.

Choose Health

With apologies to the universal society of couch potatoes, of which I am a founding member, we must move our bodies and stop eating crap. Sorry, but it's not optional: to live our fullest life, WE MUST CHOOSE GOOD HEALTH. It is the most important choice we can make for ourselves. Without it, nothing else really matters. It doesn't matter how wealthy we are, how wonderful our relationships or even how grounded we are in our spirituality if we are too sick, feeble or lethargic to enjoy them. This choice may not guarantee a life of healthy living, but it certainly increases our odds.

The first hurdle for many of us on a journey to improved health is to understand that it is a choice within our span of control. Actually, it's a series of choices we make each day. Do we eat the cupcake or the apple? Do we go for a walk or watch this mind-numbing thing on television? Each of these small daily choices will lead us to or from good health. Cumulatively, and over a period of time, these small choices add up to a big impact.

Our dietary choices have the biggest influence on our overall health. Half of heart disease, stroke, and diabetes cases are linked directly to poor diet. And that's only the tip of the iceberg. Our typical response? Every once in a while, we might go on a diet. For a few weeks, we will go on the (insert clever name here) diet, the whole time thinking about those donuts we're going to inhale when this horrible experience is over.

The next hurdle we face is the food processing industry. They tell us, "Look how we've taken this perfect food from Mother Nature and made it even better." They haven't, and it isn't. More likely they've stripped most of the essential fiber and nutrients, replacing them with refined sugar, salt and a lot of unpronounceable chemicals. In the process, they've probably concentrated the calories to make it far more fattening than nature ever intended.

Let's not forget the billion dollar fitness industry because they're not entirely blameless either. While their effect may be more benign, in most cases their messaging is not helpful. The good news, they tell us, is that great fitness is available to us but only with their assistance. And, of course, that assistance comes with significant cost and effort. Presumably without their assistance success will be virtually impossible. When faced with the choice of spending time, effort, and money with the fitness industry or doing nothing, many of us choose nothing.

I'm not saying skip the gym and do it all ourselves. I am saying choose our own path. That path may be to the gym, it may be on our own, it may be with a buddy, or it may be a combination of all those things. The key is to do it, and the message is to use the method that best suits our individual needs.

Now let's examine the truth. It doesn't need to be that hard. It certainly doesn't need to be that expensive. With a simple shift in perspective, a few changes and some minimal focused effort we can achieve significant improvements in our overall health.

The first thing we can do is move health up our priority list. The top of the list should work fine. We tend to carve out time for our highest priorities. Where do we find that time? We should probably start with our screen time, whether that screen is a computer device or a television. The added bonus is we will probably all get a bit smarter too.

Nothing tastes as good as healthy feels. This doesn't mean we can't enjoy our food, although in most cases, we need to enjoy less of it. Food is the stuff Mother Nature grows for us. In most grocery stores, we find it on the perimeter. That is in contrast to the stuff we find in the center aisles, which is often more accurately described as crap. To improve our health, we need to eat a higher percentage of food and a lower percentage of crap. It's fine-tuning our fuel mixture. The better we get at this, the more our health will improve.

Finally, we need to move our bodies more. The easiest and most sustainable method is to find or reconnect with those activities we enjoy. Walking, cycling, sports or anything that gets us moving will help. As we engage in these activities and want to improve our performance we could even conduct some support training such as the dryland or off-season training more serious athletes use. The most important thing we can do is take 10 to 15 minutes each day to crank up our heart rate. That could be as simple as a quick run or a burn on a bicycle.

Choosing good health is really choosing energy and vitality. A strong healthy body supports a strong healthy mind, and we need both to achieve maximum performance and enjoyment in life. When we have to dig deep on our toughest days, we need to rely on reserves of energy and strength to battle through like the champions we are. Always choose good health.

The Code of Purpose

PURPOSE. Our primary purpose is to be helpful, kind and compassionate. From this basis anything is possible.

Let's start the discussion of life purpose with a story. This is the story of a good friend of mine. Kevin recently passed away after living a life that was far too brief. Normally I avoid things like churches and rituals, but this one I wanted to attend. As I pulled up to his celebration of life I was puzzled by what I witnessed. Despite the large venue it wasn't standing room only, people were actually lined up out the door. I can say with certainty he hadn't cured cancer, sent a rocket to Mars or solved world hunger. What had caused such an outpouring of support?

To the casual observer, Kevin was a normal guy. He had a pretty normal day job, certainly wasn't wealthy and wasn't a community leader in any traditional sense. True, he was a dedicated family man. He had a killer sense of humor, the rare kind that would leave you short of breath with tears in your eyes. He was also an amazing guitar player, although he never achieved the level of recognition he probably deserved for his talent.

As his celebration unfolded people lined up to take the mike and say a few words. Their words told the true story of Kevin. They spoke of his love for family and friends. There were many stories of him breaking his busy schedule to help others or simply share his time. They crafted an image of a very humble, warm and kind man who connected to others naturally and never seemed to get upset. Despite his modest lifestyle, he was that guy who would give you the guitar off his back as he had to some of the people in the room.

As I left the celebration, it occurred to me that Kevin's life was the essence of living with purpose. It wasn't so much the things he achieved as the way he lived that made the difference. I believe there's a lesson here for all of us. We don't need to achieve great things in our made-up world to leave a great legacy. The greatest thing we can be is our authentic selves. If we get that part right, everything else is just a bonus.

When we approach life from a basis of helpfulness, kindness, and compassion, we are well on our way to success; however, we choose to define it. These are the attributes that facilitate deeper connections and lead to a smoother more effortless path through life. They eliminate friction, and all things run smoother when we control the force of friction.

When we apply these traits to our chosen vocations, we become much more valuable. In our own businesses, they become invaluable. Every successful business on the planet helps solve a problem for somebody and relies on strong trustworthy client connections. These qualities are the basic building blocks of successful commerce.

They are also the attributes that build and maintain our most cherished relationships. Love attracts but helpfulness with kindness, and compassion maintains. These are what build the trust, respect, and support we desire from our closest relationships. They are also great predictors of success and longevity.

Sometimes we believe the qualities of helpfulness, kindness, and compassion belong in the helping professions. They actually belong everywhere and can be even more effective in areas or sectors where they may be noticeably scarce. The more they spread across the various corners of our world, the better off we are all likely to be.

PART II

———∿∿∽⌒⊙⌒⊙⌒⊙∽∿∿———

THE ACTIONS

Learning to Change

Great, we have eight codes. Now what? We can read them a thousand times and not much will change other than our perspectives. What we need now is action because, as we all know, action creates change. Before moving into the actions it may be helpful to review the skills we use to create tangible change in our lives.

Typically, when we learn new things, we move through four stages of competence: unconscious incompetence, conscious incompetence, conscious competence, and unconscious competence. In unconscious incompetence, we have no awareness of the importance or existence of a skill, let alone how to do it. We then move to awareness of a skill with no competence to achieve it. Next, we gain competence in that skill, but we must maintain deliberate focus to be effective. Finally, as that skill becomes imbedded, we execute without thought; it becomes second nature.

Reading this book will get us to conscious incompetence. Intentionally and consistently performing the following actions will get us to conscious competence. If we stick to it, we will eventually get to the big prize; these actions will become second nature.

One of the first things we learn in the process improvement world is there are no perfect processes and all processes can be improved. The same holds true here. We are striving for improvement by degree, day over day, week over week, and month over month. Perfection is an illusion. If we aim for it, we will miss, and in the worst cases, this may cause sufficient frustration to quit.

Before moving into the action phase we can pause and choose a couple of perspectives. Change can feel like a heavy laborious grind or a light playful dance. We get to choose. This might be a good time to turn to our spirit for guidance. It will take a playful approach filled with curiosity. Let's follow the spirit on this one.

There are people who believe they can create change in their lives, and there are those who believe they just can't. Ultimately, both perspectives are correct. Now is a great time to pause and choose which of these people we will be. We are all capable of change, and it starts with our own system of beliefs.

Some of the practices will come easier than others and this will vary by person. That's perfectly normal and should be expected. For some of us quieting the mind during meditation can be a challenge. We should keep doing it anyway; we will improve. For others, it may be the practice of non-judgment that causes us to stumble. If we pause, reflect and go again, we will find the improvement we seek.

In coaching, we refer to this as the process of deepening the learning and forwarding the action. We are not only learning about the practices, we are learning about ourselves. In the space between our actions, we pause to review those things that worked and those that didn't. We can celebrate our victories before turning our attention to those areas that still need focus.

The reflection period is for asking ourselves questions. What happened? How did this make us feel? What did we learn about either the practice or ourselves? What, if anything, are we going to change next time? A journal is a great support tool for focusing our thoughts in reflection before moving back into action. It's also a fun way to review our progress as we move further down the path; it can show us how far we've come.

Let's not forget the spirit in all of this. It can help too. The spirit has been pulling us in this direction our entire lives. Most of us have been too busy to notice. When we drop our resistance to the pull of the spirit, good things are bound to happen.

Habits

We humans are creatures of habit. Over time we settle into habits and routines that become so ingrained in our daily lives they become automatic. We do them because we do them, and often without conscious thought or awareness. It's almost like we're flying on autopilot. Part of our focus in these actions will be to change old habits into new ones. To achieve this we're going to have to switch off the autopilot and get back to flying ourselves.

Autopilot has been a great enhancement to the aviation industry, but it's no way to live a life. In autopilot, we miss too much of the richness of life. We may get stuck in careers, relationships, environments, and perspectives until we have no other options. As long as we're still breathing, we have options. Finding them starts with waking up and taking control of our lives with intentional choices.

There are three classic phases of habit change. To create change, we must first identify the old habit, disrupt the pattern or routine, and then replace it with a new routine or habit. We will use these three steps as we approach the following actions. With sufficient practice, the three-phase approach becomes a habit itself. This is also a great life skill to develop.

In the business world, many of the stronger companies are focused on continuous improvement. They continually improve their products, services, and processes to be increasingly helpful to their market and to maintain a competitive edge. While this increases their market value, there is an equally important internal benefit to this focus.

These companies are also building a culture of improvement where the entire company becomes increasingly comfortable and skilled in dealing with change. These are the organizations that pivot effectively in major market shifts and tend to survive turbulence when others fail. They have built resilience into their corporate DNA.

We can build that same resilience into ourselves. As we work to improve our approach with the following practices, we will experience the same growth; we, too, will become comfortable and skilled in the art of change. We can build our own culture of improvement. Given how quickly our constructed world changes, this is another great life skill to develop.

Structures

Structures are tools we use to maintain our focus and keep us on track when creating change for ourselves. They don't need to be complex. Sometimes, the simple tools are the most effective; they're the ones we tend to use. There is a wide range of structures available to us. Here are a few we can use to stay focused on the process.

The first thing we should do is carve out some time to pursue these practices. The effective way to do this is to put it into our schedule like any meeting, appointment or task. When we hard-schedule our time for meditation, exercise or reflection we increase the likelihood of completion. The structure around time improves the discipline of action. While it may feel inconvenient at first, it won't be long before it morphs into an acceptable and manageable routine.

Reminders are other simple structures that can keep our focus on the mission. The best reminders help us to remember why we're doing all this in the first place. If our motivation flows from craving more diamond days, we could stick a diamond picture anywhere we can see it frequently. If deliberate foods choices are challenging, we could stick a sign on the refrigerator. I once had a sign on mine that said, "Nothing tastes as good as healthy feels." Printing the eight codes can also be effective in keeping us focused.

Keeping a journal is a simple structure that can keep us focused while engaged in reflection. Even if we stick to three simple questions, a journal can be effective in maintaining momentum. What did I do today? How did it go? What will I change tomorrow?

Structures are important for starting any change initiative. Schedules, reminders, and journals are three great ones to get us started. We are bound to find others along the way.

Eventually, the changes we chase will turn into habit and routines. As new habits form we can rely less and less on structures, although we may wish to continue them anyway.

The Power of Commitment

When we make a true hard commitment to change, we have no choice but to move into action. That is how we know our commitment is real; we are compelled to act. As soon as we commit, we are going to notice something powerful; the universe will move to help us. All kinds of things will become available to us. There is an undeniable heightened awareness that flows from true commitment.

Let's say we have purchased a new vehicle, a white Ford Explorer. What is the first thing we notice when driving our new vehicle home? The road is absolutely full of white Ford Explorers; they're everywhere. Did everybody run out and purchase an Explorer? No, but we did and having committed to that vehicle our awareness has increased. That same awareness applies to all commitments and can be leveraged to move us forward. When we commit, we become aware of the support around us. These are things we would have otherwise missed because we simply weren't looking.

The most important step in any worthwhile activity is the first one. When committing to our own improvement, the hardest part is stepping through the door. On the other side, we find stamina, focus, resilience, and insight. Distractions disappear, obstacles are defeated and momentum builds. Is it easy? No, but it feels that way. If we commit to the following actions, we can harness that same power.

Let's go find our diamond days.

Connection

There are three primary activities we can choose to facilitate connection. These activities help connect us to universal intelligence and/or our deeper selves. Through these activities, we build deeper calmness and clarity. As we gain competence, we begin to consider the possibility that these two entities, the universe and the self, may actually be one and the same.

Meditation

Meditation is our key process for communication with the universe. It's our satellite uplink. Through this link, we connect to the universe and, by extension, to other living things. If understanding spirituality is our primary enabler, meditation is our primary practice. Gain competency in meditation, and we're well on the road to success.

This one takes some practice. The goal of meditation is to calm the brain and empty it of conscious thought to allow a connection. Our conscious thoughts are what disrupt the connection process. In the achieved state of mental calmness, we effectively release our intentions and desires to the universe. It may help to think of it as prayer for the secular (or the religious, I don't judge).

One way to think of meditation is a gathering and leveraging of the eight codes to achieve the connection experience. When we practice meditation with non-judgment, we simply notice the process without opinion. Detachment and acceptance allow us to drop any expectation of outcome. Our intentions and desires are guided by good choices that do no harm to ourselves, others or our natural environment. Anything we seek, we are also willing to give.

My "go to" meditation practice is the one proposed by Dr. Wayne Dyer in his book *Getting into the Gap*. Dr. Dyer proposed using the Lord's Prayer as the mantra, and releasing the intentions and desires into the gap between the words (hence the title). In my case, I use the words "Our Father" to describe the general universe rather than a specific religious god, although they may be one and the same.

I prefer to lie down to meditate when I can. For me, it creates a deeper level of relaxation. Instead of music, I use the rainfall setting on a white noise generator I happen to own. If sitar music isn't your thing, I highly recommend getting a noise generator. I have also heard that the "Calm" smartphone app is excellent. The sound of rainfall is one of the most relaxing sounds I enjoy. Sometimes, I'll use the sound of ocean waves for variety.

I lay on my back, get as comfortable as possible, and close my eyes and start to breathe deeply. I focus on breathing "through" my stomach; my chest remains relatively static, and my stomach rises and falls with each breath. This creates a deeper, more relaxing breath.

As I start to breathe, I focus on the intention or desire for the day's meditation. I try to keep these to a maximum of three. With each breath, I go further and further into relaxation. After about ten breaths, I dismiss the conscious focus on the intention/desire and slowly start the mantra. I match the words to my breathing: exhaling on "our" inhaling on "Father" and so on. It is a very soft focus on the words with a pause of silence between each word. Sometimes I visualize a pebble dropped into a still pool during each brief gap. The ripples represent my intentions going into the universe. Sometimes, I stay in the silence.

If/when I detect conscious thought drifting in, I will refocus on the words, or sometimes focus on the sound of rainfall. If the thought is persistent, I might pause and deal with the issue before returning to meditation. This happened a bit when I started but almost never happens now. In total, I meditate an hour per day.

There is a clear element of reciprocity to the release of intentions and desires. It's a delicate balance of give and take. If we want gratitude and respect we should send gratitude and respect. If we seek love we send love, and if we wish to be healed we send wishes of healing for others.

We send our intentions and desires without attachment to outcomes and results. They are sent with the trust that the universe is wiser and will send back what we need, even if it differs from what we want. We accept what returns with gratitude and a knowing that things are as they should be.

With this in mind, we need to be careful about getting too specific with our intentions and desires. Sorry, but "I need a million dollars" isn't going to cut it. Help us find a path to abundance might. It's really for the universe to decide.

Time in Nature

There is something wonderfully cathartic about spending time in nature; it just feels good for the soul. We drink in the experience through all our senses and connect directly to our spiritual selves. It feels like we're taking our spirit to spend some much needed time with Dad.

This is a chance to experience our small corner of the natural universe away from our noisy made-up world of endless busyness.

When we first arrive, we may notice a peaceful stillness. The air is full of fresh aromas and clean healing oxygen. The sights are stunningly beautiful. We witness the sounds of birds and other creatures and wind through the trees or water flowing. We feel the warmth of the sun or the cooling of a breeze.

As we stay for a while, we start to notice the underlying energy. What we first view as tranquil is literally vibrating with energy. This is the energy of all living things and the same energy that vibrates within us. From the insects on the ground to the birds in the air, there is a noticeable synchronicity. It is a perfect and connected system. Our presence not only allows us to witness it, we become an integral component. We become reconnected to that system.

Time in nature is critical to maintaining our calmness, clarity, and happiness. We should make it a priority, schedule it and show up as often as we possibly can. If we can't find natural wilderness, find a park. If we can't find a park, use our backyards. If we don't have a backyard, find a tree. It all helps. It should become part of our daily ritual. And let's do it without the earbuds so we get the auditory element of the experience as well.

Time with Silence

What is really going on in our heads? Many of us don't know because we haven't taken the time to stop and listen. Or we don't do it often enough. Spending time in silence with our thoughts is an effective mindfulness practice that keeps us in touch with our internal conversation. This is our chance to sit and simply be — away from the stress, the noise and the distractions of our everyday world. We tune into ourselves and become aware of our thoughts, our creativity and any cues the universe may be sending us.

Time in silence differs from the practice of connective meditation. Here we are inviting our thoughts in rather than pushing them out. Meditation pushes our intentions into the universe. With time in silence, we listen for what comes back. In part, this is the practice that can aid us in completing that communication loop. In meditation, we may use soft music or sounds like rainfall to help clear the mind. Here we are striving for complete silence.

For some of us, sitting in complete silence can be an extremely uncomfortable experience. We should do it anyway. We can start with 20 minutes a day until we become comfortable and slowly build that time to whatever period feels most effective. As we practice, the discomfort eventually fades and is replaced with a contentment and a craving for more. It's that craving that motivates us to continue the practice.

The practice itself is very simple. We find the quietest place available in our world, sit or lie down comfortably, close our eyes and just start to breathe. If we notice any physical tension it's helpful to contract and then intentionally relax those muscles. We take ten slow deep breaths and start to listen. The mind leads, and we follow and notice what surfaces. Our mindset is one of curiosity. Although this is an exercise in being present, the mind may lead us into the past or the future. It's better to follow than to resist. Our job is to simply breathe, listen and be present.

As we practice, issues and thoughts will surface that may require further exploration. It's best to note them and stay in silence. Once we have completed our session, we can take a few minutes to write them in our journal while they're still fresh. From there we can decide what, if any, actions we will take on those issues. Time in silence should become a daily practice. As we gain competence we will notice when we miss a day; there is a certain built-in motivation to this practice.

Meditation, time in nature, and time in silence: these are the three practices that connect us to the universe through our spiritual self. Individually each of these can have a huge impact on our clarity, calmness, and overall happiness. Collectively, they are a powerhouse. These are the three most important practices we can use to achieve our diamond days. Let's embrace them, practice them, and imbed them in our daily lives.

Intentional Non-Judgment

The good news is non-judgment is pretty easy to reach. It's as simple as looking at a person or situation and deciding not to judge. The bad news is it can come back, sometimes with an unholy vengeance.

The first time I consciously tried it, I felt an immediate lightness. I realized I don't have to judge this. Hell, I don't even have to look at it. That is just a choice I make, a choice within my ability to control. That simple choice put me firmly in the driver's seat.

Staying in that seat does require some intentional focus and discipline, as it would building any new skill or habit. As with most changes it requires us to identify the old pattern, disrupt it, and replace it with a new practice. The trick with non-judgment is focusing on the identification step. The others will develop fairly quickly with some intentional practice.

Identify, Disrupt and Replace

Early and frequent conscious intervention is the key. The first thing I do is identify. I simply say to myself "that's a judgment." Sometimes I say this out loud, which can lead to some amusing moments in public. It helps to recognize our own speech patterns as they pertain to judgment. My favorite used to be, "What a (insert colorful descriptor here)." I found this helps with earlier intervention before emotions bubble up, and eliminates the chance of dealing with a runaway freight train.

We should also notice our body and facial expression. If our body is tense, we need to take a breath and lighten up. Years ago, I had a boss refer to my "patent pending pissed off look" when I was having a challenging day. We could try a smile, even if we don't feel like it. Physical changes can help the mental process and non-judgment should create calm for those around us too.

Disruption is achieved by asking some simple questions. Does this really matter to me? Eighty to 90 % of the time the answer is going to be no. The replacement practice is to set it aside and move on with our day.

For the remaining 10 to 20 % of issues, it is important to replace judgment with curiosity. Some of the questions we can use to reach this mindset might include:

- What is really going on here? Do I really understand it?
- What are the underlying or root causes?

- Are my assumptions still valid?

- What changes do I need to make to be OK with this person or situation?

The questions we ask and the process we follow should ultimately lead us to the most important question "How can I help?" This is the question that takes us out of the reactive judgment mode and into something more proactive and useful. If we can't answer and act on this question, then it was really none of our business, and we should quietly move on with our day.

The energy industry has a basic underlying safety rule. The person who identifies a potential safety hazard is responsible for addressing the hazard. Whether you're a laborer or a VP, your job description immediately includes "ensure it's fixed." It is part of the industry culture.

If we change our personal culture to include the rule "you judge it you fix it", two things are going to happen: One, we are going to do a lot less judging, and two, we're going to become more useful to others. If we have some passion around an issue great, let's roll up our sleeves and get to work. If not, let's gently set it down and quietly walk away.

Creative or Logical

Are we creative or logical beings? The answer is both. We are capable of divergent thought and convergent thought. The thought patterns are associated with different processes and actually occur in different parts of the brain. Divergent thought, the creative side, is what delivers great ideas. Convergent thought is what we use to critically judge and often kill great ideas. The problem is we're taught and conditioned to use both at the same time. Talk about conflict.

We see this conflict bubble up in corporate brainstorming sessions. We ask participants to just blurt out ideas, no matter how creative or different. We are very clear we only want ideas – no opinions or judgments. We can almost guarantee in the first five minutes somebody in the room will say, "No, that won't work." It's almost as if we can't help ourselves.

But we can help ourselves. We can retrain our minds to separate divergent and convergent thought. We can invent simple exercises to flex our creative abilities in the absence of self-criticism and doubt. Actually, any creative endeavor done for enjoyment will get us there. We can draw a picture, write a story or play an instrument just for the pure joy of it. I read of a family that played a creative game at the dinner table. Each dinner they would try to come up with ten reinventions of a common household item, a fork, a chair or a shoe. Those children were developing some great life skills.

To successfully retrain we need to add a step. We need to watch for the arrival of critical thoughts because they will show up at some point. The moment they show up, we need to acknowledge them and then send them on their way before returning to our creative activity. With a little deliberate focus, this will become an easy skill to develop. Exploring our creative side is an easy and effective method for breaking our cycle of self-judgment. In time, it flows naturally into other areas of our lives.

Imposters

In dealing with self-judgment, we can pretty much follow the same process, although we have to be more diligent in hearing and addressing our internal voice. We may need to add an initial step of addressing some underlying fears if we are feeling really stuck. Many of us believe that fear is a fear of failure, and that may be true in some cases. But what if it isn't? What if we really fear success?

We see this sometimes in people who have achieved that next level of success. They make the jump and are struck with an uneasy feeling that they don't belong, or don't deserve their level of success. It's common enough that they have a name for it; it's called Imposter Syndrome. The success that was supposed to make them happy creates the opposite effect. They are continually looking over their shoulder, fearful they will be discovered as the imposter who doesn't know what they're doing.

Perhaps we should all lighten up on ourselves; in our made-up world, we are all imposters. What we are hearing is the voice of the saboteur. If through logical reflection we identify a gap in our skill set we can do what countless others have done before us. Take a class, find a coach or otherwise focus on closing the gap. Above all, we should take some time to enjoy the ride.

I have a friend who is a former professional hockey player. In his life, he's experienced wealth and fame. He has rubbed shoulders with celebrities, flown in private jets and been invited the White House. Throughout it all, he has remained humble and genuine. I asked him how he remained so grounded through his career and in the transition back to "normal". He told me he always knew it was temporary and could end at any time. While he enjoyed every minute of it he never forgot his roots. To this day, he's one of the wisest and classiest guys I know.

When we experience moments of success, let's enjoy them and stay true to our genuine selves. We needn't worry about the duration or depth of that success. These things tend to work out as they should.

Judging Others

We reserve our most frequent judgments for other humans. We have become experts at identifying the behavior of others and pointing out their mistakes to ourselves or anybody willing to listen. We do this, even though we rarely have enough information such as the subject's internal struggle. It almost seems to be human nature. Lucky for us, it's not spiritual nature.

Unlike situational judgment, it's pretty challenging to develop a hierarchy of judgment for people. I know, I've studied the problem. Can we judge the person who cuts us off in traffic? What about murderers and politicians, surely we can judge them? What if a politician cuts us off in traffic? There are far too many scenarios and variables to track. Until somebody develops an App for that, we should follow a simpler rule: judge no one. It's not our job, and we have better things to do. We can trust the universe to keep track. Our time and energy are better focused on our own karmic debt.

People are people, and they're going to mess up about as often as we have. When faced with a choice of addressing our mistakes or the mistakes of others, let's be selfish and work on us. We have a finite supply of time and energy, and that is where we'll get the most mileage.

If my spirit is an extension of the universe (or God or Nature or whatever you choose to call it), then so is yours and everyone else's. We share that strong common bond. That knowledge alone should lead us to a place of compassion and help us all lighten up on judgment. In a manner of speaking, judging others is really judging ourselves. Let's embrace our connectivity to all beings.

When we start our path to non-judgment, we may have no idea how often we do it or the toll it takes. We are the proverbial frogs in hot water. It takes a bit of knowledge and some focused effort to turn off the heat. It is the action that creates the change. The effort is not overly taxing, but the results can be impressive. This single area of focus will help us achieve a sense of inner calm and clarity. It eliminates some "brain junk" and frees time and energy for more positive and productive pursuits. Best of all, it will make us all kinder and more understanding people.

Refuse to Defend

It can feel equally heavy and draining when we engage in defending ourselves, our actions or our perspectives. Defensiveness is the other side of the conflict equation with the added complexity of ego. Any time the ego gets involved we have the potential for a blowout. Ego-based reactions are likely to be quick and emotional, and quick emotional choices don't usually serve us well.

Often we walk away from these conversations feeling frustrated, hurt or angry. These feelings eventually give way to some feelings of regret. We may regret our emotional response or our failure to raise some of the logical points to our perspective. What is the root cause here? We failed to create enough time and space to engage thoughtfully.

If we know these situations will arise from time to time, we can do some upfront planning to deal with them effectively. It's possible and desirable to create our own framework and guidelines to deal with potential conflict before it ever happens. A little planning will help us to manage these situations with calmness, and grace.

Here is our starting perspective. We never ever have to defend ourselves; that is a choice. It may be desirable in certain situations, but it is never mandatory. We can always smile, say thank you, and walk away. Usually, that is exactly what we should do.

Our Preplan

Any good plan starts with an objective. What are we really trying to achieve? If our defense is intended to create clarity around our actions or perspectives, and those actions or perspectives were intended to create a positive impact in our world, then we may be on the right track. Even then, certain conditions should be present for any possibility of success.

First and foremost the other person must be willing to listen, and the chances of that are pretty slim. We should assume they will be as stuck in their perspective as we are in ours. The impasse is broken only when one party demonstrates a willingness to listen. Since we don't control the other party, that task falls to us. For us to have any chance of being heard we must first listen to understand the opposing position.

We may be surprised by the value we find in this approach. For one thing, there is always the possibility the other person is right. It's illogical to believe we will always be right; we are as fallible as the next person. Or the real solution lies somewhere between the two positions. There may be valuable information in this exchange we can use to improve our actions or perspectives. If not, we will gain a deeper understanding of the other perspective and its root causes. This allows us to craft a more thoughtful and effective response.

Doing this successfully requires us to create time and space. We should be prepared to claim the time and space we need to address the situation effectively. "Thank you for your feedback, I'm going to take some time to consider this. I may have some further questions if that's OK." What happened there? First, we have claimed the time we need to respond effectively. We have also demonstrated respect for the differing opinion. We let them know they've been heard, and often that's sufficient to resolve any potential conflict. We may even have recruited an ally in co-creating a stronger approach to the issue.

There may be times when walking away is not feasible. This is often dictated by the power dynamic in the relationship. We may feel compelled to stay and engage if the other party is a work superior or, god help us, a spouse. We can still create our desired time and space. We do this by asking some probing questions and carefully considering their response. Only when we have a good understanding do we respond ourselves.

With time and space, we control our egos in the conversation. With questions, we control their ego in the conversation. With the egos controlled the conversation changes. It reduces the conflict and starts to look a lot more like cooperation. Will we always reach agreement? Probably not. There will be times when we simply "agree to disagree." But we can walk away from the interaction satisfied we have made an honest effort while gaining some new knowledge about the situation or person. Often that is enough.

In Practice

The identification step is pretty easy here. Any time we feel compelled to defend ourselves we need to check for emotion. If we have any feelings of frustration, hurt or anger, we can be assured the ego is involved. We should claim all the time we need to gain control before proceeding.

Before we get there we need to ask ourselves an important question. Is this issue important enough to pull us from our current state of calmness, and grace? Probably, 80 to 90 % of the time the answer will be no. The closer we get to living the eight codes, the closer that percentage gets to 100. We can revert to our starting perspective. We gently smile, say thank you, and move on with our day.

An exception to this rule may occur when two conditions are present. If the issue is highly important to us, and we need the other person to help us achieve our objective we may engage. It's in our best interest to switch from a defensive posture into something much more cooperative. That switch occurs within us. We check the ego, drop the defensiveness, and adopt a mindset of deep curiosity.

It's a bit like dealing with objections in the sales process. Salespeople are trained to treat every objection as a request for more information. When they encounter an objection, they ask probing open-ended questions to reach the root cause before responding with a thoughtful solution. Done effectively, the process finds consensus and closes the sale. This same principle works well here. Whether or not it's actually a request for more information, this approach puts us in the right mindset to be effective.

When asking our questions, we should also have a mindset of openness. We need to carefully hear and consider the responses. There may be rich information we can use to improve our solution. Two heads are better than one, and this has been proven through countless experiments in leadership. Small groups of two or more people consistently find better solutions than the individuals within those groups. When we switch out of defensiveness and recruit our critic to assist us, we are likely to find a better solution to our issue.

Over the years, I've come to understand we don't need to win every battle. In fact, there are times when it's better to lose, even if that loss is intentional. We should always weigh the short-term gain against the long-term relationship. That relationship, both in the present and the future, can be far more important than any trivial gains from the current issue. Our future successes are often achieved with the help of people in our present lives. It's better to collect allies than victories. Not to get all "Sun Tzu" about it, but if we fight fewer battles, we'll win more wars.

Once again, let's consider the spirit in all of this. The spirit won't engage because it has no ego and is too busy having fun. It changes only when it sees the potential for harm to ourselves, others or our environment. We can defer to our spiritual side to maintain our detachment, calmness, and grace.

We feel compelled to defend ourselves for a variety of reasons. If it feels like a personal attack we can dismiss it. Personal attacks are about the attacker; they're never about the victim. It's not worth a moment of our time. It's certainly not worth our calmness or grace, and we simply can't permit an attack to pull us from a more important mission. If we're defending a mission, we can replace defensiveness with something much more cooperative and useful. There are allies and information available to improve our chances of success.

Practice Gratitude

What is gratitude and why is it so important to our clarity and happiness? Gratitude is an attitude or the absence of attitude that we bring to our daily lives. It is the opposite of entitlement. Gratitude grounds us in the present instead of looking into the future for the next big payoff or into the past regretting all the payoffs we've missed. It's a deep appreciation for all the things we have in our lives at this moment.

Whether we approach life with gratitude or entitlement it gets noticed. It elicits a reaction from our own subconscious and spirit, from the people around us, and from the universe itself. With entitlement, we create a level of friction that tends to alienate those around us. With gratitude, we create harmony within ourselves, with the universe and with those around us. Gratitude creates a smoother path through life that brings us closer to the people and things that are important to us.

Gratitude is the glass half full perspective on our world. At this moment, I'm looking out my window. It's windy, rainy and cold as ass. But I also need the rain to green up my lawn. I'm grateful to have this day at all. There is an inspiring grandeur to powerful weather, although mostly I'm grateful for the house that protects me from this cold, wet day. There are countless reasons for gratitude each day if we only take a moment to notice.

There is also an internal element to the practice of gratitude. It's a heightened self-awareness; not only do we have enough, but we are enough. It's an appreciation for the countless experiences that came together to make us who we are today. Ultimately, we can be grateful for the person we are in this moment. It then becomes an appreciation for our new starting point. No matter what the road holds from here, we are ready for the trip.

In Practice

If we've ever dreamed of winning the lottery here is some great news: we already have. Science estimates our odds of even existing at about 400 trillion to one (400 million, million to one). Comparatively, our chances of winning the 6/49 lottery are about 14 million to one; for the Powerball, it's about 292 million to one. We have already won the toughest of all lotteries; we get to experience this amazing life.

While winning the genetic lottery may be at the top of our list, there are many reasons for us to be grateful each day. It's not that we lack reasons to be grateful; it's that we fail to take a few moments and appreciate the abundance in our lives. The practice of gratitude is really the practice of awareness. It is deliberately switching off the autopilot. It is probably the easiest thing we can do to achieve our diamond days. It's also one of the most important.

Each morning before we get too busy with our day, we should take five minutes to make a gratitude list. The list can be divided into four general categories: things, people, experiences and self. This is another great use of our journals, or we can keep a separate gratitude journal if we prefer.

We can't possibly list all things deserving of our gratitude, but three to five items per category should work fine. The number is a personal choice. At the end of the day, we can review our list and decide if there's anything we wish to add based on the day's events. This can be as brief as five to ten minutes; the time spent is a personal choice. Once we have established the new habit, we gradually move into a state of perpetual gratitude. The journal becomes less important, although we may wish to continue anyway.

Once a month we can take a bit more time to review our gratitude lists. This is a chance to look for any evolving patterns or trends. Recurring themes may indicate things that are important to us. These are things we probably seek consistently in our lives. This helps us find a general direction of focus or perhaps even a career path.

There are other benefits to practicing gratitude. It tends to improve our perspective by focusing on the positives. This helps reduce stress. When we include the things we appreciate about ourselves, gratitude can improve our self-awareness and esteem. It's also a discipline that improves our ability to create change in our lives. Gratitude is a simple but important practice for improvement. Let's be sure to imbed it into our daily lives.

Giving and Receiving

When we receive life's gifts and blessings with gratitude, we are moving towards a state of grace. Grace is the effortless harmony we achieve with the people around us and the universe itself. In the ebb and flow of universal harmony, receiving is only half the equation. That which we receive we should also be willing to give. The act of giving completes the loop.

Receiving with gratitude comes with peripheral benefits. These benefits are also available to us in the act of giving. When we give with gratitude, the act itself becomes more powerful. Why should we be grateful when giving to others? Basically, we get as much from the transaction as the receiver, perhaps even more.

The act of giving is an act of joy. When we give with joy and gratitude, the act has powerful benefits for both parties. The act heals, uplifts and supports both the giver and the receiver. It tells the receiver they are important; they are loved, valued and respected by the giver. In this transaction, the giver is equally important; they become loved valued and respected by the recipient. Both lives are powerfully enhanced, and the self-image of both parties becomes much stronger.

To realize these benefits the act of giving must be genuine and without any expectation. If we have an expectation of receiving something in return, it's not a true act of giving. Any benefits derived from the act disappear. Gifts must be given without attachment or expectation to derive the deeper benefits of connection.

If we experience any feelings of resentment, we should pause and ask ourselves why. Often the cause is our perception of entitlement on the part of the receiver. We should first decide if it's perception or reality. If, upon reflection, we determine the entitlement is real we have some choices to make. We may want to address this with the recipient. We may want to find a more worthy recipient of our gifts. We may even need to decide if the person has a place in our lives. There is no external guidance available here; these are deeply personal choices we must make for ourselves.

Often the gifts we give are of our material world. Material gifts are fun and bring moments of joy. Sometimes our gifts come from a deeper place. These are the gifts of that most valuable commodity of time. When we give our time in pursuit of helpfulness kindness, and compassion, we can have a far deeper impact. These are the gifts that show our respect and support. They tell the recipient they are important and valued. They demonstrate our gratitude for that person. These are the most important gifts we can give. When we give our time in support of those around us, we move closer to finding diamond days for all of us.

Tapping Intuition

In coaching, we do a lot of work around the concept of physical geography. Simply speaking, this is developing the skill of listening to our body. Have you ever noticed if you say or do something that might be a little off you experience a physical sensation? It might be butterflies in the stomach, a feeling around the heart or our face becoming slightly flushed. That is physical geography; it's our subconscious sending us a message through our body.

Physical geography is the physical manifestation of intuition. It's the "gut feeling" we sometimes get when we are making choices. Those feelings can be negative as in the previous example, or they can be feelings of warmth and contentment when we perceive we are on the right track. The body is one of the most common ways our subconscious introduces intuition to our conscious thoughts.

Other times we get an intuitive "hit". The thought just pops into our conscious thoughts when working an issue. Sometimes these hits feel counterintuitive; they make no sense, and we tend to dismiss them and continue to labor through the issues with conscious logic. It probably happens more than we realize because our instinctive awareness is not well tuned. We might want to slow down and take a second look. We could be stepping over some important and useful information.

This is probably the prime differentiator between intuitive people and the rest of us. They listen. Their awareness is much higher than the general population. It's also much more intentional. If we recall the four stages of competence, they are in the third stage of conscious competence; the really good ones are in the fourth stage of unconscious competence. The big question becomes how do the rest of us get there?

Our path starts with the belief and understanding that we are all intuitive beings. The belief is a fundamental choice; if we wish to connect to our intuition, we must first believe in its existence. For some of us, that will run counter to a life that has systematically denied the existence of intuition. We can either labor through all that mind junk or take a shortcut. The shortcut may need a leap of faith, or it might be our first intuitive act. Believe it now, and we'll prove it later. (Say that with an Arnold Schwarzenegger accent.)

In this stage, it's important to understand we'll be dealing with an intuition saboteur. We should be prepared to deal with the internal voice as we accept the initial belief and as we experience the trials and errors of practice. As with any saboteur, we acknowledge it, greet it, and name it before gently kicking it to the curb. We can then return to our practice.

Once we've established our belief, our next step is to raise our awareness. Here's some great news: if we've been following the actions outlined to this point, we are already engaged in awareness. We have switched off the autopilot, approaching life with mindfulness and intention. We are practicing meditation. We are taking time in silence to listen to our inner conversations. These are also the key practices for raising our awareness of intuition. From this point forward, let's be sure to add awareness of intuition to our meditation and time in silence. We should also stay tuned to possible intuitive hits as we move through our day. Awareness is key.

Awareness is easier to achieve when we clear our minds. Here's more great news: most of the actions we have reviewed can aid in achieving clarity. When we drop judgment, defensiveness, along with all the associated negative emotions, we clear our path to the inner guidance of intuition. The same occurs when we engage in pure creative pursuits without the negative saboteur. These activities create inner clarity, allowing us to dump our brain junk and open our minds to hear our intuitive voices.

When we've established our belief, raised our awareness, and created inner clarity, it's time to move into practice. There's nothing magical about this step; we just start doing it. When we first practice, we may be wrong about as many times as we're right. It's best to come to terms with that reality before we begin. The more intentional we've been with our belief, awareness, and clarity, the better our results. The more we practice, the more our average improves. This is true of any skill, and perhaps more so when reconnecting with our intuition.

There are exercises we can leverage to improve our skills and improve our chances of success arriving sooner. Let's take some space to review a couple.

The first of these is blurting: we observe a person or situation with an open mindset and when we get an inkling of some feeling we just blurt it out. "I'm getting a sense of (insert feeling here) is that right?" We will receive either a yes or no in response. If it's a no, we will often get back something like, "No, it's more like (insert corrected feeling here)." This tells us how close we were and can be used to hone our next intuitive hit. It's part of "dialing in" the process of intuition.

In this exercise, it's important to listen with the right focus. We are not leaning forward with an intense concentration. We are relaxed and listening with a very soft focus. We are not only aware of the words, we are tuned into the physical cues and other elements that may not even be related to the conversation. We are also listening to our own bodies. It is a form of "reading the room". If you're a coach reading this, it is listening at level three.

For those of us uncomfortable with doing this at the outset, we can recruit our inner circle to help. We can start with some close and trusted friends until we become more comfortable with blurting our intuitive hits to the larger world. We tell them what we're trying to achieve and ask for their help with open and honest feedback.

Another way to test and hone our intuition is the unconscious choice test. There are some different versions available. The idea here is we make our intuitive choices before they become influenced by conscious thought. Only then do we study them closely to check for accuracy.

In one version of this test, we write out three to five "yes or no" questions on a piece of paper. These are big questions like should I quit my job, should I get married, or should I move to Alaska? They are also real questions that have relevance to our lives. We write them out and set them aside for a day or two. When we come back to them, we answer in rapid succession: bang, bang, bang. We then take these into our next silent reflection session, as if we have made that decision, and listen for what bubbles up. We may get an intuitive hit, or we may notice a reaction with our body.

When we rely only on logical thought, we tend to follow the herd. When we rely on intuition, we tend to find our own truth, and a uniquely personal direction that nurtures our creativity, internal happiness and success. Many of the most successful people throughout history have trusted their intuition to find unique paths. Those paths often led away from the herd and created great value for themselves and society.

When we choose to believe, raise our awareness, and clear our minds, we reopen a channel to our intuition. When we practice our skill, confidence grows. With this growth, we come to rely more upon intuition as an important life-guiding skill. In a life filled with choice, it's a great skill to have.

Mind Your Health

I debated whether or not a section on health belongs here. I went back and forth a few times before deciding to leave it in. The decision was based on my strong belief in a body/mind/spirit connection in all of us. Life just works better when we're healthy. This is a description of my personal path to better health. Hopefully, this is something here you can use.

I am not a medical or health expert. I am an expert on what works for me. By following this simple program I have seen a massive increase in energy. My mental focus is much sharper. My body is lean, strong and functional allowing me to pursue the activities I enjoy. I feel great. To be clear I did this for me. My goal was to increase my performance and vitality, not to meet some standard for body size. Before starting any health program consult a healthcare professional.

I'm the last guy to lecture anybody about health. The truth is I hate dieting almost as much as I hate working out. Sadly, for people like me, there is too much evidence linking physical and mental strength to ignore it completely.

Life happens quickly. We get caught up in our daily activities and before we know it a day has passed, then a week, then a year. If our activities fail to include some intentional focus on health our physical selves begin to degrade. The process is sneaky; we just don't notice. We also don't notice the gradual erosion of our performance, focus, and energy until suddenly they become too obvious to ignore.

We are conditioned to move away from pain towards pleasure. Broccoli does not give us the same "high" as ice cream, and sitting is much easier than running. When we sit long enough and eat enough ice cream, our health begins to degrade. As our health slowly deteriorates, we finally reach a point when pain and pleasure switch sides. Lacking energy and focus, we reach the point where we associate pain with our physical condition. Pleasure and pain are the ultimate motivators in life.

I bring it up only because my physical well-being is the foundation upon which my attitude is built. When I feel better, I do better. Higher energy and sharper focus tend to increase performance, attitude, and success in all areas of my life. I was given one body for this amazing journey through life, and it is clearly in my best interest to respect it. Possessing this knowledge and actually doing something about it are two very different animals, however.

My solution was to "trick" myself into getting more active. I started by compiling a list of activities I enjoy, including reasons I enjoy them. I managed to come up with three (I freely admit, I'm no athlete).

- I absolutely love downhill skiing. For years after my spinal injury, I was reluctant to get back on skis until friends pushed me to try again. It turned out I could ski and after a lot of practice, I got back to a decent skill level. A friend has described downhill skiing as "dancing with the universe." For me, that is the perfect description.

- I also really enjoy mountain biking (mostly double track, I'm not crazy). It provides fresh air, great scenery and time in nature that just feels good for the soul.

- I enjoy the occasional round of golf. It's a great social activity, gets me outside for a few hours, and I get to play on the biggest lawn I didn't have to cut myself.

Next, I considered the enjoyment level of these activities when I was in decent shape versus couch potato mode.

- Skiing kind of sucks when I'm out of shape. I constantly make rest stops, my turns skid a lot more, and my body is way too upright. Not nearly as fun as an athletic stance through an entire run with crisp, carving turns.

- Similarly, biking isn't much fun when I'm forced to walk easy inclines while sucking for air.
- Golf. I've never been a long ball hitter, but it gets really embarrassing when I'm out of shape. I start spraying all over the course and end up counting lost balls instead of stokes.

Connecting the improvement process to a higher purpose helped with my motivation. While I was slowly building motivation, I still needed to find my "how".

Diet

Like many people, I've tried my share of diets. The wonderful thing is they all worked, at least until they didn't. The problem with dieting, as we all know, is that when the diet ends old habits return. It's a frustrating cycle that probably causes more harm than if we'd stayed chubby in the first place.

Most research points to a dietary crisis in Western society. Not only do we eat food that is unhealthy, we eat way too much of it. Our diet now consists of foods deep-fried or infused with sugar. These days, we can even find dishes that deep-fry our sugar. Over the last 20 years, portion sizes have increased substantially. Our new normal is not normal at all.

Consider the following information from the National Heart, Lung, and Blood Institute (a U.S. government agency). Bagels have gone from 140 to 350 calories, muffins from 210 to 500, and cheeseburgers from 333 to 590. Even a restaurant turkey sandwich that once clocked in at 320 is now a whopping 825 calories. One of the worst may be plain old spaghetti and meatballs. What used to consist of 500 calories is now more than a thousand. It is little wonder we have an obesity crisis. The odds are stacked against us.

A permanent diet change is the only real way to maintain the wellness required to truly enjoy life. I'm not a big fan of health food and personally don't even enjoy a lot of vegetation in my diet. About the only way I was going to change my habits was if I could continue to eat foods I enjoy. The words "more delicious Tofu please" have never crossed my lips.

If I wasn't prepared for major changes to what I ate, then I had to control the amount. Unfortunately, I also find measuring my food to be a major pain. I was becoming resigned to a life of either chubbiness or yo-yo weight. As happens from time to time, the universe shook its head and said, "Man, this guy is never going to get it." It then pointed me to towards the practice of Intermittent Fasting.

My initial reaction was not positive. To me, fasting was definitely an "eff word." As I began to read I was also a bit confused about the actual practice. There didn't seem to be one way to do it or a definitive "diet" per se. As it turned out this flexibility was more a blessing than a curse.

The basic premise is you restrict your caloric intake to a certain period of time each day. The period varies by practitioner. Some recommend 4 PM to 8 PM, others say noon to 8 PM. Most seemed to follow a Paleo style diet, but that also varied somewhat. The one consistent comment was "eliminate sugar and refined carbohydrates as much as humanly possible." That turned out to be a challenge.

In my bid to reduce sugar, I started reading food labels. What I found was that most processed foods are infused with sugar — a LOT of sugar. I was also surprised by the types of food the industry was loading with sugar. It included "healthy" options such as pasta sauce, salsa, and canned beans. As a result, I started shopping the perimeter of the store where whole foods are displayed and cooking for myself. The food tastes as good or better, and I eat way less sugar.

I started fasting on the more restrictive 4 PM to 8 PM schedule. This turned out to be a blessing of sorts since it is virtually impossible to eat more than one meal in the four hours allowed. It only took a week or so to get used to the restricted calories. After about two weeks, I began to find the schedule a bit too restrictive, so I moved to the more manageable noon to 8 PM. Since I had already started the single meal habit, I continued with one meal and added a couple of snacks when I was feeling hungry. I also started a daily round of exercise.

- I eat when I am hungry but only between the hours of noon and 8 PM
- I guard against putting refined sugar into my body as much as possible.
- In total, I have a couple of snacks and one main meal per day. (Through some trial and error, I found a mid to late afternoon meal works best for me.)

- My main snacks are bananas usually with a bit of almond butter. To my palate bananas are delicious and filling. They're also easy on the budget.

- I cook a lot of single-pot meals on the weekend for consumption through the week. (Cooking for myself is the easiest way to eat my veggies and keep sugar out of my diet. Single-pot is the easiest way to pretend I can cook.) Eggs are another great option.

- Bread is NOT a major food group. I tend to eat it only if I have a burger (full disclosure: a double burger), and that happens, maybe, once every week or two.

- Drink water.

- Use common sense, and get medical advice if you need it.

PLEASE NOTE: I have read of some studies that suggest Intermittent Fasting may not be as beneficial for women and may be harmful in some cases. Women, in particular, should consult a physician before starting any fasting program.

Exercise

Like dieting, I have tried almost every piece of fitness equipment or program known to humans. I learned that home fitness equipment is a great place to hang clothes when your dryer malfunctions. Seriously, I have owned climbers, rowers, treadmills, stationary bikes, universal gyms, free weights, and a myriad of other devices. They all worked, at least until I didn't.

As with my diet, I had to rethink my approach to fitness. I started with my overall reason for fitness because looking better wasn't working for me, and I needed a reason that was more internal and personal. By connecting a workout to activities I enjoy, my reason became a simple "be more functional."

So, my criteria for an exercise program included the following:

- It had to be effective without taking a lot of time.
- It had to support weight management.
- It had to promote functionality and enjoyment of other activities (mostly legs and core).
- It had to be easy enough that I would continue to do it.
- It had to flexible enough to do at home or traveling for short periods.

I usually start my exercise with a brisk ten to 15-minute walk. Since I exercise in the mornings, this gets the blood flowing and clears my head for the day.

Tabata

Tabata training was developed by Japanese scientist Dr. Izumi Tabata and falls into the HIIT (High-intensity Interval Training) category of workouts. Through his research, Dr. Tabata discovered an ideal interval to maximize fat loss and increase endurance and anaerobic capacity. Each Tabata lasts four minutes and consists of a 20-second work phase followed by 10 seconds of rest. This is repeated eight times. Although it started (I believe) with a stationary bike, any type of exercise can be used to perform a Tabata.

I do my Tabatas on a stationary bike because I happen to own a stationary bike (actually, it's a stand that converts my road bike into a stationary) and cycling is one of my enjoyable activities. I do a total of three Tabatas, separated by 30 seconds of full rest. This gives me a total Tabata workout time of 13:30. I try to do them every day because, as sick as this sounds, I have grown to enjoy them. More specifically, I have grown to enjoy how I feel when I'm finished.

For reasons perhaps only Dr. Tabata understands, the workout feels more difficult than if you worked the entire four minutes. Each cycle stacks on the last. By the eighth, I am gassed. It's important to work at maximum intensity to gain the full benefit. Thankfully, my maximum intensity improved considerably over the first few weeks.

There are plenty of free Tabata timers available for smartphones, tablets or notebooks. Because my bike is in my office, I use the free notebook version at tabatatimer.com. Otherwise, search your app store.

I have pretty much divested myself of all home exercise equipment for the simple reason that I don't need it to get an effective workout. With the exception of the bike, everything I do consists of simple bodyweight movements. As with any exercise program, you should consult a physician and learn how to do them properly to avoid injury. There are many resources online that cover proper body movement.

The most important movement I do is a simple body-weight squat. It's excellent for core and leg strength needed to perform well in most activities. I started slowly, completing only 25 squats my first day. Over eight weeks, I slowly built this up to 175 squats. Today, I do 175 squats in approximately five minutes or less. I know I could do more, but this achieves my goal of functionality in a short workout.

Next, I move on to some core. I mix these up a little depending on the day. Some days I do simple sit-ups, and on others I do Russian Twists or planks. I spend about three to four minutes per day on my core.

Finally, I do some pushups to maintain some upper body strength. This is another movement I started slowly. In the first few weeks, I did them from a knee position before carefully moving forward (I have been susceptible to shoulder injuries in the past).

And that was my entire workout. It lasted nearly 35 minutes. Later, when I moved into more of a maintenance mode, I cut this time to between 23 and 28 minutes by alternating squats and core every other day. Following my exercise, I try to do some simple stretching, mostly for my hamstrings, quads, and groin. Sometimes I will do these for a few minutes through the day when I have free time. I stretch to the point where it feels good but never to the point of pain.

Here are some things I did to maintain the momentum:

- I kept my reasons for change in front of me to remind me why I started.
- I tracked progress daily with a spreadsheet that included a weight chart. Even though weight

Made in the USA
Middletown, DE
17 January 2019

wasn't my primary purpose, it was the easiest thing to track.

- On my low motivation days, I made a commitment to start. For some reason, when I took the first step to exercise, I always finished.

- If I just couldn't find that first step, I didn't beat myself up for missing a workout. I made a stronger commitment to ensure I didn't miss two in a row.

- I focused on the endorphin high I got from the workout (mostly from the Tabatas).

- I understood going in that there would be setbacks. Preparing ahead of time seemed to make it easier to shrug off.

It helps to think of food more as fuel than a pursuit of pleasure. That doesn't mean you can't enjoy it, just enjoy less of it. Eating is still largely a social activity in my world. It's easy to go out and enjoy a meal with friends. I simply make sensible menu choices, like sticking to water

and usually avoiding a large dessert. I keep in mind; this is my daily meal, and I move my snack times if needed.

This section could have been called the couch potato's guide to fitness. It is as minimalist as I could find to achieve a reasonable level of health and fitness. It provides an excellent base for enjoying outdoor activities or adding new ones. One day I hope to push my physical condition further. I would like to try things like yoga since I have heard such great things about it. But for now, I am functional enough to meet life's challenges. And if my "one day" never comes I'm not going to beat myself up over it.

Primarily I owe my success to two things: Intermittent Fasting and Tabatas. The simplicity of this approach has worked well for me, and you may find the same. If it doesn't don't get discouraged. The process can be as important as the result. Try out some different things and seek help to find success. I guarantee it is worth the effort.

Purpose

There is a ton of advice floating around our world that suggests all manner of methods for finding our life purpose. I want to put this as diplomatically and spiritually as I possibly can: much of it is not helpful. This advice usually sends us on a path to find something we absolutely love to do. That's as likely to be a treadmill as a path. It can lead to a lengthy search filled with exhaustion and unhappiness until one day we realize we're right where we were when we started. We discover all jobs suck sometimes, even when we work for ourselves.

Other experts will tell us to find something we're good at doing. We were born good at two things: cycling food and breathing. Everything since we've had to learn. We get good at things when we focus, learn and practice. We get good at jobs by doing them, so that doesn't really help us pick one. After a while, we are good at a lot of things, but that doesn't necessarily mean we want to do them.

Sometimes doing the thing we're good at doing becomes the most boring and unfulfilling thing we can do.

Others will advise us to do something that pays. That's decent advice but doesn't really help us with focus. We can make money at pretty much anything. There are people making big money playing video games on *YouTube*. There's not a lot we can't make money doing these days. The other common advice we see is to do something the world needs. Again, not bad advice, but the goalposts move daily on that one, and it's a pretty long list already.

All this advice has the same fatal flaw. It assumes we have all the time in the world, and that simply isn't true. Time is our most precious and finite commodity. We should guard it, respect it and use it wisely. In respect for our time, there is a better way.

Let's pick a direction that supports our values, do a quick intuition check and go. We'll figure it out along the way.

The secret is not in what we do but how we do it. Some of the most enlightened people on the planet are engaged in housekeeping or gardening. They're called monks, and they achieve fulfillment by maintaining an internal focus.

With an internal focus, we approach the work with pure gratitude, not only for the job but for the paycheck at the end of the week. We put in maximum effort and completely immerse ourselves in the work. We take the opportunity to learn everything we possibly can. We are helpful and treat our coworkers with kindness and compassion. We accept the occasional "suck" or learn to treat it with detachment. We stay positive and become that person with whom others want to work. We become valuable, even indispensable. We stand out, and only then do we get noticed.

We build our legacy, the world starts to notice and opportunities begin to surface. Maybe we get promoted, maybe a client or competitor makes an offer, and maybe we take

our skills to an entirely different sector or head out on our own. This starts our path to a higher meaning and purpose. Even though we haven't looked for opportunity, it has found us, and that is the fundamental universal truth in all this.

When we stop looking for our next great opportunity, it has a better chance of finding us. The future focus distracts us from the work we need to do today, and it's the work we do today that prepares us for our future. It gets us noticed, and compels those around us to reward our focus and achievement. We control what we can in the situation; we control ourselves, our focus, our engagement, our gratitude, and our attitude. We stay alert and let the opportunities reveal themselves. Instead of finding something great to do we have found a way to be great, and nobody can take that from us. Throughout the experience, we remain helpful, kind, and compassionate.

PART III

———∿∾◦∾❀∾◦∾∿———

THE WRAP-UP

The Eight Codes

1. DUALITY. When we build our universal awareness, we find calmness, balance, and confidence. In this state, we make better choices.

2. CONSTRUCTS. There is no right or wrong way to navigate the world of human constructs. We can make our own rules.

3. NON-JUDGMENT. When we practice non-judgment, our lives become lighter and

freer. We have time to pursue more productive things.

4. DEFENSLESSNESS. When we refuse to defend ourselves to others, we find calmness and grace.

5. ACCEPTANCE. We are right where we should be. Be grateful and present.

6. DETACHMENT. We are much more than our transitory wealth or bestowed titles.

7. CHOICES. When we make choices through filters that do no harm to ourselves, others or our environment we find harmony. Always choose good health.

8. PURPOSE. Our primary purpose is to be helpful, kind and compassionate. From this basis, anything is possible.

The Actions

CONNECTION. We achieve connection with our deeper selves and the wider universe through the practices of connection meditation, by spending time in nature, and by spending time in silence with our thoughts. We should do all three daily.

NON-JUDGMENT. We achieve non-judgment through intentional focus. When we replace our old habit of judging ourselves, other people and most situations our lives change. We drop brain junk and achieve clarity for more productive pursuits.

REFUSE TO DEFEND. We can replace our defensiveness with a simple smile and a "thank you". When we intentionally remove the ego, we can change the conversation to be more cooperative. We can recruit our critics to find better solutions.

PRACTICE GRATITUDE. Gratitude should become an intentional daily practice that eventually morphs into a state of perpetual gratitude. It keeps us present and deepens our connections with others. We should bring gratitude to the acts of giving and receiving to enhance the experiences.

INTUITION. Finding our intuition requires us to believe in its existence. We then increase our awareness and clear our minds to focus on the physical and mental cues of intuition. With deliberate practice, our intuition grows.

PHYSICAL HEALTH. Achieving good health will be as simple or difficult as we choose to make it. Good health flows from good choices to eat cleaner food and that will allow us to move our bodies in effective and enjoyable activities.

PURPOSE. We can find purpose and fulfillment in any activity with the right internal focus. When we engage

with gratitude, helpfulness, kindness, and a learning mindset we increase our value to the world. When we are more valuable, the opportunities tend to find us. Instead of finding something great to do, we have found a way to be great. That is ours to keep.

Connected Themes

There are some connected themes running through this book in much the same way they run through our lives. It may be helpful to pause and review a few of the more central ones. A little clarity never hurts to drive the message home.

When we change ourselves, we change our world. Our journey is less about what we do and more about who we become. We become positive influences in our own corners of the world, and sometimes even role models. Our internal focus influences how we interact with the world around us. We become intentional with where and when

we expend our time and energy. This all transforms how we experience our own reality.

We can view our world through many different lenses. Each lens creates a certain level of distortion based on our personal beliefs, values or biases. Through one lens, we might view our world as the physical things we can see and touch. With this lens, the real world is primarily a world of human constructs.

Through another lens, we see the physical world but consider the possible existence of some higher power. The world is still the physical world we can see and touch, but behind that world is an entity or power that may or may not be real.

Then there's the lens that starts to flip that paradigm. This lens sees the world behind our physical world as real, and our physical world as often fabricated. There are certain advantages to viewing our world this way.

There are things available here that can ease our path through life.

People with this lens are inclined to believe they have been given this life to experience, and they're here to be; their purpose is to experience a great life with pure gratitude and to help those around them with that experience. They feel no pressure to build wealth because they believe wealth is largely fabricated and temporary. The abundance they receive is more often used for tools, not jewels. As a result of this detachment, they have less stress, higher awareness and general feelings of contentment.

They are also inclined to live their lives without expectation. They are in a state of acceptance; they live in the present because that's where they get the richness of experience. They are intentional with their choices, and those choices are often about when and where they will interact with the physical world. They view judgment and defensiveness as distractions, and simply refuse to engage. And

while these things are available to anyone who chooses them, this lens tends to make them feel effortless.

Awareness

We achieve our desired changes through increased awareness, mindfulness, and intention. Change is virtually impossible to achieve without first shutting down our autopilot and taking control of our lives. This allows us to control or detach from the negative influences in our lives and turn our attention to the positives.

With awareness, we are capable of controlling our own judgments and detaching from the judgment of others. Awareness grounds us in the present, the only dimension where life occurs and allows us to experience true gratitude for everything we have in this moment. It enables us to make better intentional choices and connects us with our intuitive power to improve the choosing process.

Choices

Life is choice. The story of our lives is primarily the story of the choices we've made and the consequences that flowed from those choices. Virtually everything we do in life starts with a choice. We choose the things we do, the things we think, and the things that merit our attention. Logically, when we improve our choices, we improve our life, and this is probably our most overlooked truth.

Understanding this truth sets us on a path of raised awareness that makes us much more intentional with our choices. We switch off the autopilot and bring a higher focus. We come to understand the process of choosing is a skill like any other. It can be sharpened and focused through intentional practice. Through this focus, we make better choices that enhance our lives and the lives of those around us.

Once we've made a choice, we move into action; we need to execute. A choice without action isn't a choice, it's a wish. It only becomes a choice when we move in our intended direction. We take as much action as possible immediately following the choice, and before we've had a chance to talk ourselves out of it. If this isn't a central theme in our lives, we should make it one.

Mortality

Before leaving the area of themes, here's one final uplifting thought: we are all going to die. Each and every week over one million souls will depart our planet Earth for destinations unknown. That is an entire large city just gone. Here's the weird thing: none of us believe we'll be one of those people. And we will do almost anything to maintain that belief or avoid that entire conversation. Maybe we should do the opposite. Let's not avoid the topic of mortality; let's embrace it. Let's explore it, understand it, accept it and use it to build better lives.

To understand mortality is to understand time or at least time as it pertains to our own lives. Our time here is finite and blows by very quickly. How finite? Nobody knows, but just to be safe maybe we should get our important stuff done this week. Our schedule might be tighter than we know.

That is the power that flows from embracing mortality. When we're on a tight schedule, we tend to get things done. It shakes us out of our complacency: our awareness is higher, we develop a laser focus, and we create a sense of urgency. We are much more present. We are driven to pack more living into our days.

I once worked with an engineer who had an interesting philosophy, at least for an engineer. His simple motto was "Tuesday is the day to get shit done." And he would; he would tear through an amazing pile of work each and every Tuesday, spending the rest of his week with the finishing touches. Even though he did most of his weekly

work on that single day (or because of it), he was the highest achiever on the team. He understood the power of a tight schedule. For the rest of us, today might be Tuesday; let's get shit done.

It's not only getting things done, it's getting the right things done. We humans are a bit obsessed with being remembered after we're gone. The tributes occur in the ritual held after our departure, a funeral or celebration of life. Here's something you won't hear at those rituals. "We are gathered here today to remember Bob. Bob drove a Cadillac and had a cottage up in lake country." Pretty silly, right? It's silly because those are the unimportant details of Bob's life.

Bob wants to be remembered for the lives he touched, the people he helped and the positive impact he had on his world. If Bob is remembered for those things when he reached his destination, then Bob focused on those things along the journey. Let's be more like Bob; let's focus on important things.

Possibility

When we look past the limiting boundary of human constructs, we become aware of the vast potential that lies beyond. Other than our obvious constraint of time, our lives are wide open worlds of pure possibility and potential. We are the explorers in those worlds. These are vast worlds filled with all existing knowledge, and knowledge yet to come. It all exists for our enjoyment and exploration.

Our current realities are tiny constructed micro-environments occupying no space in an infinitely larger galaxy of potential. Let's lighten up, break out and go play. Who knows how much fun we'll have, what we might discover or how much bigger our lives may be.

Higher Plane

Imagine this: we are sitting in the universe's most comfortable recliner. In our hands is a bucket of the world's

tastiest popcorn, and in front of us is the world's clearest big screen TV. Playing on that screen is the world's most intriguing story; it's our life, and we are watching in total fascination. The best part of this scenario? It's a mystical screen, and we can step through it whenever we choose to become immersed in that story. As deliberately, we can step back to the recliner and continue watching. It's our choice, and we are in complete control. There is no remote; we do it solely with our minds.

When we approach life from a higher plane, we get to choose when, where and how we engage with our world. We can engage fully with all those people and issues that are important to us, and detach from the distractions that bring no meaning to our lives. We focus higher energy on the important by wasting none on the mundane. That is a very powerful thing. It makes us much more effective and builds our clarity, confidence and overall happiness. From this place, life feels light, playful and often effortless. It is rich with diamond days.

Optimal Performance

And while there are clear benefits for living well, there are also some exciting implications for performance. In this state is the ability to develop a laser focus and stay on our mission. There is the ability to maintain calmness under pressure, and sustain a higher level of energy. There is the ability to improve cooperation and make better decisions and plans. There is the confidence to execute on those plans in the absence of doubt. The implications for personal performance are significant.

What would be possible if we pulled together a team of like-minded individuals and asked them to create? What could they achieve? What ripples might they send through our world? The implications for teams are even more exciting.

Coaching

We can achieve our diamond days by intentionally practicing the actions suggested in this book. Of that, I have no doubt. If we want to move faster or dive deeper, we may want to consider the assistance of a coach. While not necessary, it can certainly be helpful. Every person on the planet could use a little help from time to time, and the wise ones admit it.

I have experienced coaching from both sides: I have coached, and I have been coached. Coaching can be a powerful and transformative experience with one critical caveat: both client and coach must be completely and intently engaged in the process.

If, as clients, we aren't prepared to invest the time and effort to create our change, I have a better idea. We should take our coaching money and buy an Xbox; it won't change our lives, but at least we can escape it for a few

hours. Otherwise, we should come to every coaching session prepared for total engagement. It can be a fun experience filled with discovery, learning, and growth but, like most things in life, we have to show up and participate.

We should also take some care in choosing a coach. The coaching sector is still a bit like the Wild West; there aren't a lot of rules or regulations. To put it charitably, skills can vary widely from coach to coach. At minimum, choose a coach with a certification from a recognized school of coaching.

If you decide to try coaching and are struggling to find a well-qualified coach, I can probably help you. I am connected with a wide network of excellent qualified coaches around the world and can point you in the right direction. Look for me on the internet or various social media sites.

Author

Paul Chapin has worked with countless teams and individuals over his career as a business and personal coach. He is trained and certified by the Coaches Training Institute of San Rafael California. He is a Certified Professional Coactive Coach (CPCC) and holds a Master of Business Administration (MBA) from Athabasca University.

Paul's unique coaching style draws from a 20-year executive and management career developing employees at all levels. He is an acknowledged process expert with experience identifying systems and patterns and converting those patterns into simple and useful processes. This ability has become a central theme in his coaching practice. He is dedicated to finding simple paths through complex issues.

An avid skier and cyclist, Paul spends much of his free time in the Canadian Rocky Mountains. He coaches, writes, and consults from his home base of Calgary, Canada.